G000165554

A Very Quiet

BY THE SAME AUTHOR

A Bad Day for the Sung Dynasty (1984)

The Intelligent Observation of Naked Women (1987)

Ridiculous! Absurd! Disgusting! (1989)

All published by Carcanet Press, Manchester

A Very Quiet Street

Frank Kuppner

Polygon
EDINBURGH

© Frank Kuppner 1989

Polygon
22 George Square, Edinburgh

Set in Linotronic Sabon
by Koinonia, Bury
and printed in Great Britain by
J. W. Arrowsmith Ltd
Bristol

The publishers acknowledge subsidy from the Scottish
Arts Council towards publication of this volume

ISBN 0-7486-6004-6

'Is West Princes Street a very quiet street? — Yes.'
MARGARET DICKSON or M'HAFFIE

'I was going up West Princes Street, which is invariably a very quiet
street.   WILLIAM CAMPBELL

'That is a very quiet district and a quiet street.'
EUPEHEMIA CUNNINGHAM

'It is particularly quiet at night, about seven o'clock.'
CONSTABLE FRANCIS BRIEN

It is a very quiet street. I have seen the old lady several times at her
window; I do not know that I have seen her moving about.'
ROBERT BROWN BRYSON
from witnesses at the trial of Oscar Slater. May, 1909.

M & L

Introduction

This book, an investigation of some aspects of the Oscar Slater case by someone with an accidental but close interest in the matter, is written in such a free manner that anyone who did not already know the outlines of the story would have extreme difficulty in following it. I have therefore added this introduction, hoping it will be sufficient to enlighten those utterly innocent of this sorry business. Readers who are well up in the background of the case may ignore it if they wish, for I am fairly certain I will not reveal anything in it which is not also mentioned in the body of the work. Yes: I think that is fairly certain. (On the other hand, I am promising nothing.)

*

At 7 p.m. on the 21st of December 1908, a servant-girl left her mistress's house in 49 West Princes Street, Glasgow, to go to buy the evening newspaper. On her return, ten minutes later, she discovered her downstairs neighbour waiting outside her door, attracted by loud noises which he and his sisters had heard from the old lady's flat immediately above them.

The servant-girl unlocked the door and went in, moving across the narrow hallway towards the kitchen. As she did so, a man suddenly appeared from a lobby by the bedrooms at the other side of the hall. He walked politely up to Adams (the downstairs neighbour, still standing at the door), who since Lambie (the servant-girl) said nothing, and the man himself seemed affable, suspected nothing. The man reached Adams, passed him, and only then broke into a run down the three flights of eight or so steps leading to the street.

Lambie went to investigate the area the man had come from, near the kitchen, and only then came back to enter the dining-room (the door to which was the nearest to where Adams still stood), where she had left her mistress earlier that evening. This person was an 83 year-old spinster called Marion Gilchrist. Miss Gilchrist was lying on the floor, with a rug over her face. Her face had been beaten in with extraordinary force. A doctor who lived across the street (first interesting but irrelevant tremor: he too was called Adams) was fetched, and he arrived, examined the scene, and telephoned the police. Under police instruction, Lambie made a thorough search of the building and reported that a valuable diamond brooch was

1

missing. (A small box had also been broken open, and some papers and letters had been scattered on the floor. (Miss Gilchrist had a liking for costume jewelry, and her house at the time of her murder contained thousands of pounds worth of such valuables.))

The police issued a description of a man wanted for questioning, based on the descriptions of Lambie and Adams. Two days later, a 14 year-old message girl called Mary Barrowman came forward to say that she had been passing 49 West Princes Street at the time of the murder, and that a man had come running out of the said building, passing very close to her. She gave a highly detailed description which differed considerably from the Adams/Lambie version, and both descriptions were then circulated within the police-force, with a caution that the two men may be connected, but should not be confused with each other.

Four days after the murder, a bicycle dealer named Allan MacLean called in at a police station to report that a German Jew, whom he knew only as "Oscar" had been trying to sell off a pawnticket, taken out on a diamond brooch, in a card-playing establishment called The Sloper Club. He took the police to where he knew the man lived, a fine redbrick tenement close by at 69 St. George's Road, five minutes walk away from the Gilchrist house. Enquiries were set in motion.

A Detective Powell was sent to 69 St. George's Road to find out what was what. Calling at a door nameplated Bernstein (attracted, for all I know, by the German-Jewish name, but still getting the wrong person—a precedent perhaps?), he learned from the Miss Bernstein that lived there, and her servant, Ruby, that the description of "Oscar" tallied closely with that of a man in an upstairs flat, the door of which proclaimed him to be one "A. Anderson, Dentist".

Powell returned to base, reported what he had found, and, late that night, was sent back to St. George's Road in the company of two other detectives, with orders to arrest this man, whatever he was called, unless he could reasonably explain his whereabouts on the night of the murder.

The door of the Anderson flat was opened by a servant-girl, known as Catherine Schmalz. She was another German, and one whose command of English was a little on the basic side. She seemed to deny that any man was living there. The police were given permission to search the flat, and, in doing so, they discovered a piece of wrapping paper addressed to, "Oscar Slater, Esq., c/o A. Anderson, Esq.", which gave them for the first time the surname, or at any rate a surname, of their suspect. A further enquiry to Schmalz elicited the fact that "he is away for a holiday with Madame".

From some of the ever-helpful neighbours, a Detective Millican

2

learned that Slater had left, in the company of a woman, at 8 o'clock that very evening, which was only an hour or so gone. (The new description of a wanted man, derived from Barrowman, had appeared in that evening's newspapers.) Powell's first visit had been at about 7 o'clock. It is rather a pity that, for whatever reason, he had not managed to find his way to the correct door. Superintendent Ord of the CID gave instructions that all south-bound trains were to be watched.

When a Detective Lieutenant Gordon returned to Slater's house on the following morning, Schmalz told him she thought he had gone to London, along with Madame Junio, a Frenchwoman, with whom he lived. (Slater was indeed married, but to someone else.) It was discovered, by a detective visiting Glasgow Central Station, that two single tickets for the 9.05 train to London had been sold that evening to a man fairly closely answering Slater's description. Information from the woman who had been got in to take over Slater's lease on the Glasgow house (a Mrs. Freedman) suggested that their ultimate destination was Monte Carlo.

Schmalz, who had been given a week's notice on the 21st, travelled to London, which she had left only a couple of months before, with Slater and her mistress, for Glasgow. The London police interviewed her, learning among other things that Slater was in permanent flight from his wife, and that his destination was in fact America—but that he wished the possibility of Monte Carlo to be given out, to throw his wife thoroughly off the scent. The end result was that Ord in Glasgow received a telegram informing him that Slater and Junio had left from Liverpool, intending, ultimately, San Francisco.

Inquiries were made, and the Liverpool police discovered that a couple exactly answering the description had left for New York on the 26th of December, travelling under the alias of Mr. and Mrs. Otto Sando. At the request of the Glasgow police, these two were detained on arrival in New York, and extradition proceedings were initiated.

Lambie, Adams (the neighbour), and Barrowman were all brought by ship to America for these proceedings, during which the two females positively identified Slater as being the man they had seen, and Adams testified that Slater was "not at all unlike" the man. But in fact judgement as such was never given in this suit, for Slater, who had by now been in custody for nearly 5 weeks, stated his readiness to return to Glasgow of his own volition, and there face the charges preferred against him. This he duly did.

By the time Slater was brought back to Scotland, in February 1909, the Glasgow police were in possession of statements from

3

numerous witnesses, all variously testifying to the presence of a youngish man loitering noticeably in that area of West Princes Street directly surrounding Miss Gilchrist's house. (This man is usually referred to in the literature as "The Watcher".) Over a dozen of these eye-witnesses took part in identification parades involving Slater, and all of them identified Slater, and did so subsequently at the trial.

This trial took place over 4 days in May 1909. At the end of it, the jury retired for 70 minutes—Slater remaining in the dock all that time, apparently supremely confident of acquittal (to begin with, at least)—before returning and pronouncing him, by a majority, guilty. (Nine for guilty; five for not proven; one for not guilty. A simple majority convicts.) In the pause occasioned by the practice still current at that time, of copying out at length the charge and subsequent verdict (it took in all about seven minutes—the practice was changed as a result of the Slater case), Slater proclaimed his innocence, in baffled and vehement terms. He was sentenced to death.

So: where do we stand now? We have a somewhat unsavoury foreign drifter found guilty of the cold-blooded and appallingly brutal murder of an 83 year-old woman, committed in pursuance of an attempt to steal her valuable jewelry. There is no evidence in mitigation: no history of insanity, no blackmailer in the wings— nothing of that sort. And yet, midway way through the three-week gap between sentencing and execution, a petition for clemency signed by 20,000 people was sent to the Secretary of State for Scotland. Two days before the date when execution was due, Slater's sentence was commuted to life imprisonment.

*

Perhaps some of the following considerations played a part in this commutation:

The brooch which Slater had pawned, which first brought him into the case via MacLean the bicycle dealer, had been originally placed in pawn several weeks before the murder. It was, thus, not Miss Gilchrist's brooch at all. Indeed, it was of a markedly different design. (All this was testified to at the trial.)

No evidence was led to show how Slater could have learned of the existence of Miss Gilchrist's jewelry. (The Lord Advocate, for the Prosecution, in his final address to the jury, specifically promised to address this point at a later stage of his speech, but he in fact never returned to it.)

No evidence of any sort was led to show how Slater could have got into a house protected, in all, by two doors and three locks,

4

which showed not the least sign of forcible entry. (Miss Gilchrist's timidity was testified to. Adams had in fact been alerted on the night of the killing by what he took to be three loud knocks against the ceiling—Miss Gilchrist's floor. This was a "help" signal which had been agreed between them, should the old lady meet with an emergency.)

For weeks prior to the murder, it had been Slater's publicly expressed intention to leave Glasgow in the near future. His actual departure, between the two visits by the police, occurred openly, before any new description was put out in that evening's newspapers, and involved a porter who had been hired even earlier, to help transport nine carefully packed trunks. (The Lord Advocate, in his final speech, talked of "a flight from justice" caused by his name appearing in the newspapers. In fact, Slater's name did not appear in print until early January.)

At the New York proceedings, Helen Lambie had said unequivocally that she had not seen the intruder's face. At the trial in Edinburgh, she said she had.

In New York, both Lambie and Barrowman testified to the intruder (Lambie) and escaper (Barrowman) wearing the same type of coat and hat, and being the same man. It will be recalled that their earlier descriptions were so different that the police notice itself specifically warned against confusing the two men. (In fact, Lambie abandoned her earlier description and embraced Barrowman's. The two girls also shared a cabin on the twelve day trip to New York. Barrowman testified at the trial that they had not discussed the case at any point.)

Before the proceedings in New York, Barrowman, Lambie and Adams were all shown by the police a photograph of Slater'the very man they were there to identify.

Barrowman and Lambie happened to be standing with a Glasgow police officer in the corridor in the New York building, directly outside the door through which Slater was led in, to take part in the extradition proceedings.

At these proceedings (in New York) the witnesses heard the evidence given by the other witnesses.

Numerous photographs of Slater appeared in domestic newspapers from January the 13th onwards. Slater was continually identified as the Watcher by people who had seen his photograph.

Slater was an obvious foreigner, in dress and appearance, strikingly unusual in Glasgow 1908. However, no witness ever suggested the Watcher (or the Intruder, come to that) looked like a foreigner when they first saw him—except for a police witness who, on his own evidence, mistook him once in the street for someone else! But

5

at the trial, numerous witnesses agreed that he was the only obvious foreigner in the identification parade offered to them, and they all picked him out as such without difficulty.

A young schoolteacher named Agnes Brown was included on the list of Crown witnesses for the trial, but she was not called to give evidence. Her story is that, on the night of the murder, she was passing down West Cumberland Street (the first turning left on West Princes Street, moving west from its commencement at St. George's Road—this street is now called Ashley Street) just after 7 o'clock; and as she was passing into West Princes Street, two men passed her at a run, and continued on down that road until they reached Rupert Street (the second turning on the right from that point), down which they disappeared. The significance of this can be appreciated when it is compared to Barrowman's evidence, according to which one man ran away, and turned left up West Cumberland Street itself. He would thus, of course, have passed Brown. (The situation is complicated further by the fact that, although one of the two men described by Brown possessed the "long grey overcoat" originally testified to by Lambie (and always by Adams), Brown, at an identification parade, unhesitatingly picked out Slater as being the *other* man. It is thought that this may be what prevented the defence from calling her.)

Barrowman testified to following the fleeing man a little way down West Princes Street, before turning back westwards to continue on her errand. Yet neither Lambie, nor Adams, nor Adams' married sister—nor anyone else likewise out on the street very soon after the flight—testified to seeing *her*, nor she them.

The murder was presented as having been carried out by means of a lightweight domestic hammer found in Slater's luggage on his return from New York. No clothing was found in the nine suitcases corresponding to the clothing of the alleged Watcher. The inference is that he got rid of the clothing, but carefully kept the hammer. (The expert prosecution witnesses would not swear to there being any blood on the hammer.)

Lambie and Adams disagreed even about so basic a point as, where Lambie was when the man emerged. According to Adams, she was several steps into the interior of the house. According to Lambie herself, she was still at the door, beside Adams.

Lambie's identification of Slater in New York was not straightforward. In fact, when asked if she saw in the room the man who had walked past her that night, she replied: "One is very suspicious, if anything'. She gave several further instances of what could easily be taken as a reluctance to go on.

Adams, who had the best and most sustained view of the intruder, at no point actually testified to a positive identification with Slater. (Despite this, in his final address to the jury, the Lord Advocate claimed that, in effect, he had.)

The most striking feature of Barrowman's original testimony which was extraordinarily well-detailed given the circumstances, was her reference to a "twisted nose". This was soon domesticated to a "nose slightly turned to one side (thought to be the right side)". Slater had a long nose which had been broken at some time in the past, but the peculiar adjective "twisted" could be applied to it only as a result of rather intense special pleading. (Barrowman's description gave a profusion of detail which would have spoken well of her powers of observation had it been of a stationary figure in a bright light. In fact, it was presented as being that of an unexpected fugitive rushing pell-mell through an ill-lit street. She was able even to give a colour to his boots.)

Barrowman's identification of Slater in New York was not straightforward. First she said, "He is something like the man I saw." She then altered this to, "He is very like the man I saw." At the trial itself, she was certain as to identification.

All the witnesses of the night of the murder spoke to seeing a clean-shaven man. At that time Slater had almost a two-week growth of moustache.

Slater bought tickets for Liverpool, not London. A porter testified that all his pieces of luggage had the destination stickers, Liverpool, on them.

Slater had left his wife four years before, and had soon after taken up with an Andreé Junio Antoine. This woman was not a vestal virgin, and Slater was undoubtedly a gambler, and a man who lived, one might say, on his wits. However, at the trial, when the defence witness, Hugh Cameron, was asked, "What he [Slater] was?", and, replying, "He was a gambler," was further asked, "Anything more?", he made the devastating reply: "Yes, I had it that the man, like a great number of those who came to Glasgow, lived on the proceeds of women." This was very damaging as to Slater's character, but was, of course, self-admittedly sheer hearsay. However, both the Lord Advocate ("a life which descended to the very depth of human degradation") and the trial judge ("a man with the prisoner's sinister record"—in fact Slater had a proven criminal record of two minor misdemeanours for affray) seemed to accept it as established. The intrusion of this unjustifiable hearsay can, at the very least, hardly have helped Slater.

And, of course, in England such a hung jury would probably have resulted in the prisoner's release.

*

Small points, perhaps, but possibly one or two of them gave a sensitive mind cause for reflection. However, whatever the reason for their lordships' decision was, they did not choose to share it with the base and vulgar. Slater was sent to Peterhead Prison, and there, still ungratefully insisting on his innocence, he began his life sentence.

*

In April 1910, "The Trial of Oscar Slater" appeared in book form, edited by William Roughead for the "Notable Scottish Trials" series. This consisted of a transcript of the trial, a few relevant appended documents, and a long introduction which drew polite attention to certain of the more bizarre aspects of the case.

The publication of this book alerted the wider reading public to the fact that something very strange was going on. However diplomatically phrased, the introduction clearly suggested, and from an unimpeachable source (Roughead was himself a distinguished Edinburgh lawyer), that the verdict was, to go no further, not an inevitable consequence of the evidence led. This widening of the interest in the Slater case, as involving something more than merely a sordid little local murder for minimal gain, eventually brought the facts of the case before Sir Arthur Conan Doyle, the creator, inter alia, of Sherlock Holmes, who did not take long to reach the (to be frank, utterly obvious) conclusion that Slater had nothing whatever to do wi£1.29 murder. A small inexpensive book of his, entitled "The Case of Oscar Slater", came out in 1912.

It was Conan Doyle who refocussed attention, among other things, on the curious behaviour of the burglar; who neglected several prize jewels that lay readily to hand in the spare, unused bedroom where Miss Gilchrist kept her valuables (and to which the intruder apparently went quite without hesitation), and instead broke open a document case and scattered its contents over the carpet.

It was also in 1912 that a high-ranking officer of the Glasgow Police Force, a Detective Lieutenant Trench, began taking home official files of the Slater case to study, and, in some instances, to copy out. This man, the holder of the King's Police Medal, was one of the best detectives in Scotland, and of such value that Glasgow frequently lent him out to help with tricky problems in outlying areas. He later communicated his thoughts in the matter to a Glasgow lawyer named David Cook, who wrote to the Secretary of State for Scotland, informing him that an as yet unnamed policeman had fresh and controversial evidence in the Slater case, but that he feared to bring it forward, it being a criminal offence for a policeman to divulge information received in the course of duty to anyone not a

8

member of the force. The Secretary of State eventually wrote back, promising to give the matter his fullest attention.

This information was such as to make an Enquiry inevitable, and one was duly convened in April 1914 to consider Trench's allegations. These, in essence, were that Helen Lambie, when she visited Miss Birrell (a niece of the deceased) at her home just round a corner halfway down West Princes Street, within ten minutes of the murder taking place, did not content herself merely with revealing the brutal fact, but also identified the man whom she saw leaving the house. That this had, from the first, been known to the police, but that those at the head of the investigation, deciding that Lambie was mistaken, had taken care to suppress all mention of this, to protect an innocent man in an extremely invidious position.

Trench produced documents purporting to be contemporary signed statements by Lambie and Miss Birrell to this effect. He had also fortified his case by making copies of various documents in the police files, complete with page numbers.

At the Enquiry proper, one witness after another stated Trench's submissions to be utterly untrue, including Lambie and Miss Birrell. Under the conditions of the Enquiry, witnesses (who were not put on oath) were interviewed individually by James G. Millar, the Sheriff of Lanarkshire, in the presence of a clerk. Transcriptions were then prepared and signed. Witnesses were not confronted with each other. Contradictions were let through without demur. Documents (other than Trench's) were not required to be produced.

Guided by the findings of this Enquiry, the Secretary of State for Scotland decided that no further action in the Slater case was necessary.

Trench was suspended, then sacked. In 1915, he and Cook figured in a trial of their own, on a charge of reset preferred against them by the Glasgow police. The circumstances of this prosecution were so anomalous that the case was dismissed at once, without a hearing, and both men were released. Trench died in 1919, aged 50. Cook died in 1921, aged 48.

In 1925, as the result of a personal appeal from Slater, smuggled out on a pellet of paper by a released prisoner, Sir Arthur Conan Doyle applied again to see the Secretary of State for Scotland, pointing out that Slater had now been in prison for 16 years, (which was longer than the norm for life sentences), and asking whether it would not be possible for him now to be released on license. The reply ruled this out.

In 1927, a Glasgow journalist named William Park published a book entitled "The Truth About Oscar Slater". Power had been a friend of Trench, and was given much encouragement by Conan Doyle, who was in fact instrumental in having the book published. In essence, this work was merely a concise, forceful restatement of what was already known, although a certain amount of new material was added. But it requires truly heroic powers of obtuseness to read it and not be convinced that Slater had nothing to do with the murder of Marion Gilchrist.

The publication of this book led to further journalistic activity, which served to vindicate the conclusions of Power's work, and the government now decided, as a humanitarian gesture, to release Slater, who had spent eighteen and a half years in prison.

This, however, was not uniformly well received. Pressure for a full-scale Enquiry grew, and, in July 1928, Oscar Slater's appeal was heard before five law lords. This was considered on four principal points: that the verdict was not supported by the evidence; that additional evidence had come to light; that available evidence had been withheld at the trial; that the judge's final summing-up to the jury contained misdirections in law. The appeal was *rejected* on the first three counts, and upheld on the fourth. In the light of this, Slater, no longer the proved murderer of Marion Gilchrist, was awarded £6000 compensation from His Majesty's Government, out of which he had to pay his own costs.

Slater remained in Scotland until his death, in Ayr, on February the third 1948, at the age of 75. February the third happens to be the date of birth of my younger sister, but, after all, one must be born, if one absolutely must, on some day or another. Another coincidence, and one which drew me far more forcibly to these events, is the fact that , in 1951, I myself was actually born in the neighbouring house to the one where Miss Gilchrist was murdered.

(The following notes are given as they were written, in chronological order. Statements tendered in one section, may thus be altered, corrected, withdrawn, forgotten about, etc. in subsequent sections.

Italics are usually for emphasis. However, entire sentences printed in italics are later observations added during the process of preparing a printed version of the text from manuscript.)

One

Let us follow him, then, as he climbs the reasonably presumed steps to the police station. I suppose he does not halt during his climb, and consider the possibility of going back home quietly and letting the matter rest there, or find its own level without him. After all, the newspapers have talked of a brooch stolen from the house of a murdered old lady, and a foreigner whom he perhaps finds unsavoury or dubious has been offering to sell his interest in such a brooch in a club which they are both members of. (The usual suggestion is that this object was haphazardly picked up by the murderer just before leaving, from a collection of similar pieces, to suggest theft as a motive—a silly and desperate move which turned out to be hysterically successful. (What thief would break a jeweller's display window, and remove a single plain ring from the periphery of a vast, expensive haul? It is perfectly possible, of course, but, unless the thief is mad, it can hardly be called simple theft. But the thief might have been mad. (But when the police arrested someone who was obviously not mad, and insisted that he was a thief. I suppose there are indeed many stupid thieves, or thieves who behave irrationally.)) Yet we should also, I think, keep in mind the possibility that the brooch never even existed. (We have only the word of a single, drastically unreliable witness—Lambie—that it was missing from its accustomed position in the first place. Or, if we have insufficient reason to think that Lambie invented the brooch, since it would be unjust to assume that she lied from sheer force of habit, we may think that, in the turmoil, she did indeed discover the brooch to be absent from its accustomed position. And then, perhaps a day or so later, she remembered what had become of it—or she may even have found it, say, unexpectedly attached to one of the dead woman—s dresses (and, if so, she has a choice, does she not? Admit her mistake, and incur the wrath of so many people, or keep or dispose of the brooch. Very likely none of this happened, but, if it did, I think we may assume she had not a split-second of doubt about what she would do. (Good God, who would notice yet another ill-described brooch. Perhaps one of her relatives is still wearing it. Or threw it away decades ago as an object of no value, of whose history she was entirely ignorant.) *(In fact, a jeweller testified at the trial to the existence of the brooch in question. Its whereabouts, however, were to the best of my knowledge never resolved.)*

11

He has therefore, as a good citizen, no choice, whatever his personal wishes, but to continue manfully up the stairs and into whichever police-station it was, to give them his utterly worthless bit of information. (For how would he subsequently feel if it were to be discovered that the brooch was, in fact, the right one. (Or if time passed, and there was no progress made in the search: particularly if he found out, as surely he would—yes, as almost certainly he would—that Slater had left, bag and baggage, for America, within two days of the killing?)) After all, what harm can come of it? More to the point, if it were discovered that Slater's brooch could not possibly be *the* brooch (which was discovered at once to be the case), to what sane man would it even for a moment occur that the police might somehow surmise that, through presumably the direct intervention of Providence, the man involved in this trivial coincidence would turn out to be the killer anyway, despite the fact that there was not a single other material clue connecting him with the crime? Truly, one feels that, if the wife of the Lord Provost of Glasgow had been observed wearing a similar new brooch, the detective branch would, with equal aplomb, have decided that they need look no further. I should say so. Strange that, if he had paused at the top of the stairs, thought better of it, and returned to his modest abode, unwilling to get himself involved in such a business (as presumably did many other members of the Sloper Club, India Street, who also knew that Slater had been offering to sell a pledge for a brooch, but who, for one reason or another, did not share this priceless information with the police) Slater would probably have died in America, on a day when millions of others also died, utterly unheard of. But he opens the door, and goes in, and Slater dies, memorably, in Ayr. (Nothing more, I think, is heard of this MacLean.)

Two

Slater's alibi is at once prosaic and fascinating, and would surely be
some indication of innocence, were it not that the possibility of being
guilty never even arises. (That is one of the fascinations of the case.
A man came very near to hanging, and served, what, 18 years in
prison, for a crime which it is not possible for a second to believe
he was responsible for, even though the actual culprit remains
unknown. How could the police possibly believe it was him? There
was, I think it may be said, once the false trail of the brooch was
cleared out of the way, absolutely nothing to connect Slater with
the case, except for the fact that he lived in the neighbourhood.
10,000 other men could have been found guilty with as much logic.
And, indeed, even the fact of his living nearby (the sole indicator of
his guilt, except perhaps for his height, which was dead average (his
weight, age and appearance all contradicted the original descriptions
gathered from the witnesses)) loses some of its gloss if we recall the
electrifying testimony of the attendant at Kelvinbridge Subway
Station, about twenty minutes away from the scene of the crime,
that a man hurried through the turnstile without buying a ticket,
roughly half an hour after the crime was committed. The spotlight
picks out the killer (or perhaps one of the two accomplices) for a
moment.

(Perhaps. I am fairly sure that nowadays retribution from the
authorities would be immediately forthcoming, if one tried to leap
the electronic barrier. Kelvinbridge is at present the nearest station
to where I live. (Interestingly, and it occurs to me only as I am writing
this, the closest station to the scene of the crime is the next one down
the line, at St. George's Cross, reachable very quickly from Miss
Gilchrist's, in under two minutes at a sprint. (I should know: it was
the station nearest to the house where my family lived for the first
16 or so years of my life. I remember the street well, in its previous
incarnation. (It was being devastated for developmental, traffic-
centred reasons around the time that we left.) The station was tucked
in a corner, formed where the facade that lined the road suddenly
dived back to create a pavement twice as wide. It was a curiously
dark, mysterious little spot as I recall it, and I doubt if, structurally,
it had changed much in the 50-odd years intervening, for all the
X-million to-ings and fro-ings up and down the very steep, irresolute
stairway—several of which manoeuvres, for all we know, may have

been made by the murderer himself. (Was there anybody standing on the platform at the time of the murder? Almost certainly. And yet we will never know his, her, or their names—who are, after all, part of the story. Perhaps, had the murderer chosen a straighter course, they would have solved the problem at once. And so we probably *still* wouldn't have heard of them, since the case would sink back among all those appallingly straightforward murders, which it seems almost a crime itself to be interested in.)

No doubt the murderer did not choose that station, as it was altogether too near. Or, no doubt, by the time he could think straight he was nearer to Kelvinbridge anyway—although, if he had been thinking *really* straight, he would have paid for his ticket and become utterly immemorable, unless 7.30 in the evening was not as busy a time then as it is now.) But I would be interested to know what would have happened if a ticket-collector had asked to see his ticket. After all, this man had (probably *(actually it is far from clear that the man at Kelvinbridge had anything whatever to do with the case)*) lately committed a murder, probably without premeditation. It is likely that his response to a challenge would have been interesting.) But the man disappears unsuspected, and no-one notices the station at which he departs the train. Doubtless, wherever it was, it was conveniently placed for access to the house of at least some of the now deceased spinster's estranged relatives. (Which reminds me that I must try to find out who benefitted from her will.) The judge however seemed to take the view that this personage tied in well with Slater, who took advantage of his great good fortune in living close by, by running to a comparatively distant railway station, presumably to brood over his doings on a journey the long way round the circle back to St. George's Cross.

(Slater was seen standing outside his home within an hour of the murder by a witness passing by. This witness was not called at the trial. Perhaps Slater merely took the short journey back one station, to St. George's Cross? The judge seemed almost to take the view that Slater was such a blackguard that he did not deserve to live, whether he was guilty or not; but he might as well be found guilty for neatness's sake.))) Slater's alibi was, that he was having dinner at home at the time of the murder. It is unfortunate for him that he had invited no guests, for a single pillar of the establishment, there for whatever (I grant you, implausible) reason, would surely have killed the case stone dead. But his (more or less) wife was there, and her maid; and although the judge chose to believe the latter's admission that her mistress sometimes received gentleman visitors in the evening ("gentlemen" here presumably meaning nothing more than "male"), and based on it some disgraceful remarks in his summing-up, which eventually had the proceedings overturned on a technical-ity as a mis-trial 19 years later, he chose not to believe her testimony as to this modest, normal, familial meal. But, of course, it is as certain as anything in this case is that it really did take place. One more meal, as innocent as most, (what happened to the wife after the trial?—disappeared, I suppose); a few bites taken as a nearby door is opened; the plate nearly cleared as a nearby chair is lifted. (And intervening doors opening and shutting all the time. (Including some doors of the house where I was brought up. Who lived there then? Who was in the room where I was actually born? Is all this gone?) And chairs without number were being subtly rearranged—some brought closer to the fire, some moved slightly for ease in many places in a little procession of meals—and one now lying on a floor, soaked in blood, while its neighbours still stand by, in their previous attitudes of innocence.) They finish the meal, talking normally. His life will soon be shattered. They rise from the table and go into another room.

(In my rereading the next day, I learn that the fleeing passenger in fact flung down the required penny fare onto the ticket-counter, and thus did not defraud the Underground cashier of its legitimate revenue. But he did not stop for long enough to pick up his ticket (as, I suspect, legally required to do for the transaction to be a valid one), and thus he was still as open as ever to challenge by an inspector making an impromptu swoop (one chance in two? in five? in ten?) on the train in which he was travelling.)

Three

How much, or how little, can I recall of the circumstances under which I first heard of Slater? I am fairly certain it will have been in the kitchen of the top-floor flat in West Princes Street where I lived from birth to mid-teens. (Not having been there for the last 20 years, I can nonetheless remember its lay-out fairly exactly, including the large recess in the wall to the right of the small entrance corridor from the door, doubtless originally for a bed, but now neatly accommodating the huge family table. (On the right of the kitchen-door was the door to a large cupboard. On the left that of a smaller room within which occurred the earliest events of my life which I know myself to remember.

(I remember standing in a cot beside the cot of my elder sister—both were ricketty wooden affairs, supported by what seemed to me then to be high legs—and I was jumping up and down. (It was not clear to me in my recollection why I was jumping up and down (I think I assumed it to be sheer youthful high spirits and thought no more about it), but a few months ago I happened to mention this to my mother, and she, after an expression of surprise that I still remember that (somehow I had assumed that everyone must know I remembered it) told me that it was a favourite pastime of me and my sister to jump up and down in our cots, as we thereby managed, thanks, I assume, to the natural tilt of the floor, to travel some way across the room, towards the window.))))

I do not remember the circumstances of the discussion (after all, one talks confidently for decades, convinced that someone somewhere must be writing down what is being said, of such immense interest and importance is it), but at one point my mother broadened out the subject a little to mention that a famous murder had once been committed two doors away down the street. This seemed to us children (although who "us children" exactly were, I forget) to be a bit too good to be true, (possibly only myself and my elder sister again, (it can hardly have included, in any receptive sense, my younger sister (and I have a brother too) who was born sufficient years after me, for me to have a fairly distinct, albeit mystified, recollection of that event also (of not being allowed into the kitchen, of strange comings and goings (no-one had told me anything, and I had no more notion of what was happening than if, well, than if a murder was being committed)). I mention this largely because it is

16

my sister's 29th birthday in two days time, and I have just put a card to her in the post-box on my way to the library this afternoon, half an hour or so ago, after phoning up my mother in her house on the west coast to find out my sister's new address in Edinburgh, which, we can add with confidence, is on the East Coast.), but my mother insisted that such was indeed the case: that a famous murder had once been committed, just down the road, and (I think she added) that a man who had not been responsible for it had nonetheless been imprisoned for a long time. She then remembered that, when her husband ("your father") had just acquired the renting of the flat, she had written as much, very naturally, in her latest letter to our uncle who was living in England, and in his reply he had hoped that it wasn't the Slater flat. But no, she repeated: the Slater flat was two doors down the road. (One self-sufficient main door flat intervenes.) After which, I cannot remember hearing him mentioned for years. (Actually, the next clear recollection that I have is of mentioning this modest coincidence to someone who worked in the BBC building by the Botanic Gardens. He proceeded to tell me that his own father had been at the trial (!). (Apparently, as far I recall, he had returned home, distraught, after the verdict.))

Four

It is, I trust, not too callous to point out that Miss Gilchrist, who was either 82 or 83 when she died, was, despite being the victim of an appalling and fatal attack, possibly the longest-living of all those who had anything to do with the case. (Slater himself, for instance, was 76 when he died, exactly twice the age he would have achieved if the law had taken its initially appointed course. (Indeed, for all we know it may even have been her sheer persistence in living which, by annoying someone, led to her demise.)) But if, say, three months earlier, she had fallen victim to a normal minor ailment of the aged, she would be no more to us now than any other of the little old ladies who must have died in West Princes Street, of whom nothing else whatever is known. And Slater too would have led a different life, and no doubt we would not know about him either: not that he visited Glasgow in 1901 (as did millions of others—it was the year of the Great Universal Exhibition in the city); or in 1905 (for obscure motives, like so much else in his life); or in 1909 (for a brief stay of two months before travelling on to, or so he supposed, San Francisco). But now we learn that, when the body was first discovered by Lambie, and, shortly thereafter, Adams, she was not yet dead. She made a final movement of her left hand. (Having reached her early eighties; fond of jewelry; unmarried; puzzlingly wealthy; a magazine abandoned for a moment still lying face-down upon the table). If, even an hour earlier, she had simply fallen to the floor dead, without cause from elsewhere. If she had died, even in an appalling agony, we would have learned absolutely nothing about her. She could have writhed through a thousand devastating movements of pain, as no doubt others did, and we would still have heard nothing, seen nothing, and imagine nothing. We do not know, for instance, how the people died who were in the rooms of my house then.

(To revert to MacLean for a moment. *(In fact, he testified at the trial.)* I might mention, as I have since discovered, that, of the £200 so generously offered for the apprehension of Slater, this M'Lean received £40. It is difficult to work out quite how the portioning-out was arrived at, but I feel M'Lean would have had legitimate grounds for feeling aggrieved. It is true that he did not know the brooch-dispenser's surname, having only nodding acquaintance with a foreigner called "Oscar", yet, without him, where could the police possibly have begun the search that would lead them triumphantly to Slater? (Can we assume he was horror-struck when Slater was finally released? (I must try to find out if he was still alive then.)))

Five

Of Miss Gilchrist it may with some certainty be said that no part of her life is as well-documented as her dreadful death. Indeed, our knowledge of her previous 82 years in their entirety seems to come to far less, in precision and exhaustiveness, than our knowledge even of her fatal injuries. Simple arithmetic suggests her year of birth was 1826. Do we know where, or do we simply assume she was born in Glasgow? (Perhaps a dozen significant buildings already existing in that era still survive in the city.) It is odd to think that, while Beethoven dies in a thunderstorm in Vienna, some presumed parents are presumably cooing with half-disbelieving wonder at her first approaches to speech. Presumably the same rain cannot be falling. Or that, in the next year, as Schubert tries to find a way to lie at rest comfortably, not yet even dreaming that his illness is fatal, she has presumably mastered the art of walking. At this time, one trusts, her strange devotion to jewelry has not yet begun to manifest itself. (Of late, by the way, I have been desultorily reading Sir Walter Scott's journal. (Indeed, now that I think of it, the edition which I bought a few months ago (there seems to be no modern edition) was dated 1898 or some such year (certainly, late nineteenth-century)—published, that is, when both Slater and Gilchrist were alive (and Mary Barrowman was a very young girl of three or thereabouts, beginning to walk, talk, invent stories, etc.); the former not yet having visited Glasgow, the latter already an old woman of 70-odd, who had lived in West Princes Street for 20 or so years by now, and whose death in her sleep, need I repeat, would not have been the cause for much concern or comment anywhere.) I have not yet finished the book, but it is a little eery to consider that, doubtless on one of those myriad days when the good-hearted author spent eight or so hours in the library writing well below standard more or less non-stop (his day enlivened only by a long walk, or a couple of hours of jovial tree-felling) Miss Gilchrist put in her first appearance in the world. (I at length went over to the book-case, and found the requisite volume. There were no "Gilchrist"s in the Index, as there easily might have been, so normal is the name. It transpires that the date of the publication was, in fact, 1891, which affects all that I have already said so little that I need not bother changing it, since they were both alive during all those days anyway.) But by 1870, or 1871, when Slater was born (or rather, when an Oscar Joseph Leschziner was born in Oppeln, Germany, with whom it could reasonably be supposed that a Miss Marion Gilchrist of Glasgow would never have the least communication, be it the merest passing glance (and it seems likely that, in fact, they did not, although perhaps Leschziner once saw a little old lady on the other side of St. George's Road (or, perhaps more accurately, possibly she passed through his field of vision once))), we may, I think, assume that some sort of interest in expensive costume jewelry on her part had already made itself known. After all, she may have been 44 years old. (It was, more or less, the time of the Paris Commune. Perhaps, occasionally, she had begun to read an article about it in a magazine, but had had her attention distracted to something else—a knock at the door perhaps—had folded back the magazine, placed it face-down upon a table, and moved away. She may also have placed her spectacles down at its side, if she already wore spectacles, which is possible.)

Six

Pursuing a little further the question of Miss Gilchrist and the architecture of Glasgow, we may remark that Blythswood Square, which is the only typically Edinburgh square to be found in the Western Metropolis (by the Edinburgh architect, John Brash) was begun in 1823, when Marion Gilchrist was not yet conceived, and was completed in 1829, when she was probably walking (and perhaps occasionally still falling) (although on none of these occasions did anyone then climb up onto her rib-cage and belabour her 50 or 60 times about the skull with a very lightweight hammer (which, indeed, despite the utterly ridiculous amount of time expended on this possibility at the trial, never happened at all)). Blythswood Square is still locally notorious as being the site containing the house in which the family of the architect Joseph Smith (1806-63) lived—a minor figure, but one responsible, for instance, for the workmanlike facade of the Treron building in nearby Sauchiehall Street (still there, passed by thousands every day (as surely Miss Gilchrist must time without number have passed it. (As surely must, in the 1860's, perhaps on the same side of the road as her, a locally domiciled doctor named Pritchard have done, who was hanged in 1865 for poisoning his utterly innocent wife and mother-in-law)). Indeed, I have walked past it time without number myself. *(And, in the last few months, I have often walked past its burned-out shell, gutted by a fire towards the end of 1986. Apparently the intention is to save it.)*

The family house is not, however, revered as a temple of the vital art of architectural design. It is to one of the architect's daughters, a dark decisive girl called Madeleine, that the locale owes its fame. She became involved in an illicit affair with a foreign gentleman (but this time French rather than German (remarkable how the European orientation of Scottish life surfaces everywhere (actually, he was from the Channel Islands, but a Frenchman all the same))), who became troublesome and a burden to her. She gave him cocoa to drink at some of their nocturnal trysts, and he died of arsenical poisoning. (She had of late been buying precisely this poison herself as a beauty treatment. (The trial of Madeleine Smith—she was, of course, acquitted—was the first of the four great Glasgow murder trials which occurred over half a century. All these murders took place within 10 minutes walk of Charing Cross. Slater's was the last.

22

(Even though Miss Gilchrist was ten years older than Madeleine Smith. One wonders what her comments on such a scandalous subject were at the time of the trial. If she made none, she was possibly the only Glaswegian who didn't do so.) It is, I think, fair to say that in only one of them (Pritchard) was the murderer convicted. In one, the murderess (Smith) was found Not Proven. In the other two, guilty verdicts were indeed found against the accused, but, rather unfortunately, in neither case was the person thus sentenced to death the murderer. (Well, no legal system is perfect. And neither of them was actually hanged. (In one of these cases, the probable murderer was known by name, but, as he had acquired legal immunity through his role as the chief prosecution witness in the trial which found his accessory guilty (!), he could not himself be prosecuted, and thus escaped scot-free. His accessory after the fact, totally innocent of the murder, served ten years, so at least justice was partly seen to be done. The Slater case would seem to give additional weight to the principle evolved here that it doesn't much matter exactly who goes to prison for a major crime, so long as somebody does. Slater's case would seem to suggest that this person need not even have anything to do with the matter—although, of course, it is an advantage that he should live nearby.))))

I should add that quite a few people still believe in Smith's innocence. (I myself have been delightfully belaboured by one such.) This seems to me to be curious. (All the more so in that apparently, the 15-man jury which acquitted her found 10 for Not Proven, and 5 for Guilty. (In other words, no-one on the jury thought she should be found Not Guilty. We should note here that the voting in the Slater case was: 9 for Guilty; 5 for Not Proven; 1 for Not Guilty. (Decision was by simple majority—which is, I suppose, logical enough, if somewhat stark. (8 Guilty, 7 Not Proven—condemned. 7 Guilty, 8 Not Proven—acquitted. (Quite what, say, 5 Guilty, 5 Not Proven, 5 Not Guilty would be entered in the accounts as, is a question (like 7-1-7) which I have thought it better not to pursue, if only from the fear of losing a delightful fantasy.)

I have gazed at the photograph taken at the (Slater) trial: looking at the jury as if I might be able to see which of them was the wonderful man who found for Not Guilty, (the jury were out for 70 minutes in all—4.55 pm to 6.05 pm, 6 May 1909), but of course that is not possible. Allow me, nonetheless, to blow a kiss in roughly the direction of the heavens, as an inadequate expression of gratitude. (Note, please, that if merely two more had found for Not Proven, Slater would have been acquitted—7 Guilty, 7 Not Proven, 1 Not Guilty. (Of course, ideally, for the last twist of the knife, 8 rather than 9 should originally have found for Guilty. (My earlier fantasies, I now

23

realise are rather slight things. If a majority finds for Guilty, then such is the verdict. In the absence of such a Guilty majority, the accused is acquitted anyway, under whatever designation.)) (It seems to me, by the way, that three or four of the jury (I do not possess a copy of the illustrated transcript, and can only consult the one in the Mitchell Reference Library) bear a definite facial resemblance to Slater. It looks like almost pure chance that Slater is being tried for the murder, rather than one of them, for they all (I assume) had as little to do with it. (Well, I assume the murderer is not sitting on the jury, although he may be in nor near the court. I mean, they are all Edinburgh men, or so I believe.)))))

Another point about Smith comes to mind. Although she nourished her superfluous lover with cocoa of her own inimitable preparation in Blythswood Square, their relationship commenced a year or so earlier, when the Smith family still lived in its previous house, which, if memory serves me correctly, was in the reasonably nearby India Street. (This street still exists, a short thoroughfare in a curiously overlookable location, but both of its sides are now devoted to monolithic modern buildings, and not a fragment of the old architecture that I remember remains. (Yet, even as late as 1968 things were entirely different. In the summer of that year, before going on to university, I worked for several weeks of casual labour in a hotel in that street. It was an old building (albeit with a hole in the ground for its immediate neighbour), and across the road stood old tenements. (I remember once being sent across the road with a tray of tea and biscuits, to take to the youngish hotel manager, who had a flat there. As I was climbing the fine stairway in the common close-mouth, one of the girls who normally worked at the reception desk or in the offices passed me quietly in the opposite direction. (I also remember quite clearly standing in one of the dark basement rooms of the hotel, and looking out at the railings above and beyond, and the sheer frontage of the sunlit buildings on the other side of the narrow street, and the continuous succession of passing people, and being struck by a sense of what?, of how much it took to fill a large city, in this street that I had known nothing of a week or so earlier.)) This presumably was, at least in part, the original Victorian architecture.)) Now, curiously, the club which Slater belonged to, and inside which he offered for sale his pawn-ticket for a valuable brooch, which so lingered in the memory of one Allan M'Lean, bicycle dealer, was also situated in this India Street.

Seven

As the subject has been delicately touched upon, it might be best for me to deal at once with the question of my sources, and get it out of the way as far as possible. I recently (five or six weeks ago) wrote an article on the Mitchell Library in Glasgow (now, since the addition of its new extension, apparently the largest public, unrestricted reference library in Europe) and so the following impressions are fairly clear in my mind. The Mitchell Library was founded in 1877, following the terms of the will of an eponymous tobacco merchant, Stephen Mitchell. After 40 years it had outgrown its cramped central location (in Ingram Street, I think) and a new building was contructed to house it, in North Street. (One minute's walk from Charing Cross.) The foundation stone was laid by some local worthy whose name I have more than once read on the inscribed slab near the elaborate old entrance, but I have usually walked blindly past it, and I could not even attempt to guess his name with the least likelihood of success. This was done in 1907. At this time, Miss Gilchrist was still alive, over 80 years old, living five or so minutes away in West Princes Street, among her habitual neighbours. (In fact she had an additional neighbour. 49 West Princes Street, where she stayed, consisted of two flats, one on the first floor, one on the second. (It was then more usually known as 13 Queen's Terrace, even though the building was quite clearly not part of the stretch of West Princes Street which directly faced Queen's Crescent, slightly to the west (West Princes Street proper stopped just before Miss Gilchrist's house, which initiated a direct continuation of buildings one storey less in height: when construction continued later on the further side of the crescent, the name West Princes Street was taken up again, and retrospectively applied to Queen's Terrace too.) The ground floor was part of a house reached through another door entirely. The internal stairway led, first, to the floor where Miss Gilchrist stayed, and then to the top floor above her, where, at the time of the murder (the Mitchell Library, by the way, being now already partly in appearance) there was an empty flat, vacated a few months previous by, as I recall, a minister of the church, who had lived there in 1907. (No upstairs neighbour to worry about. The old lady, when the servant left, utterly alone in that close. What an opportunity! (One theory has it that two men were involved—the one who so calmly walked past the witnesses, not dripping blood—and another who had already left , either to the roadway, or to the shelter of the floor above. (I doubt very much this use of the floor above, but it is too resonant to be ignored.))))

At this time, of course, Slater was also still alive, but (like most people) not in Glasgow, although he had already visited the city twice, and, indeed, a witness at the trial would testify to the clear memory of having seen him (more than once?) during a previous visit, in Grant Street, where he frequented a club. (Grant Street is a shortish street which runs parallel with the first long block of West Princes Street. Miss Gilchrist, looking out her bedroom window, would see the back of a row of tenements across two brief back-gardens, separated by a lane. Those buildings were Grant Street.)

By the time the new library opened, in 1911, Miss Gilchrist was dead, and Slater was in Peterhead Prison. I have not investigated the circumstances of the opening, but I imagine that a great crowd was, rightly, there, and numerous dignitaries, and that soon the dead old lady's surviving relatives and neighbours began to use the inestimable resources of the building. Indeed, so central is it to the process of information-gathering in Glasgow, that it is difficult to doubt that the murderer himself used it, and the more sensible question is, how often?

(The other major Glasgow library is the Stirling's Library, from which books may actually be borrowed. This is a superb work of the Glasgow architect David Hamilton, incorporating a pre-existing mansion-house. It was built in 1828-9. It is thus contemporaneous with the completion of Blythswood Square. Originally, and for a long time thereafter, it was the Royal Exchange. Indeed, Stirling's Library as such was not begun until 1863, in nearby Miller Street, in which year its architect also died, leaving its completion to others, in 1865. Curiously enough, this architect had himself been partly responsible for the surroundings of the Royal Exchange, along with David Hamilton, whose daughter he had felicitously married. It is generally thought that his death was hastened by the late trial of his own daughter for murder by poisoning, even though she was found not proven, by a majority of 10-5, five voting for guilty. By the way, Madeleine Smith's middle name was Hamilton.)

In 1980 a large new annexe was opened in the Mitchell Library, an institution which I had long been in the habit of visiting. A large separate room was devoted to the city of Glasgow. It was not, I believe, until mid-January 1985 (two or three weeks ago) that I first found myself inside this inner sanctum, known, appropriately, as the Glasgow Room. I had developed my interest in local architec-ture—or, rather, the interest I had always had had triumphantly gone from chrysalis to resplendent maturity, thanks to a couple of

26

books which I had acquired at a nearby second-hand bookshop (they were very recent works—perhaps, to look no deeper, unwanted presents soon got rid of) and I wished to pursue this interest further. (In particular, as I recall, I wanted to find the name of the architect of the Mitchell Library itself, a building which, like the slightly insane Art Gallery, and the (to me very powerful) Royal Infirmary, none of the small architectural guidebooks would even so much as mention. (I had, you may recall, just written about the library, and was curious that its noble exterior should be so little celebrated.))

While in the Glasgow Room, I took the opportunity of inspecting those books on open display, and I saw among them two copies of the transcript (editor: Harry Hodge) of the Slater Trial. This is a book which I have been meaning to acquire for years, but I had never seen a copy of it anywhere before. I forget the exact sequence of events, but, obviously, during one visit to this part of the library I must have abandoned the slim architecure section for the shelves marked (with some, doubtless unconscious, irony) "Law". I picked out the volume on Slater (published in 1928, after the successful appeal, and read the 70 or so pages of introduction before the transcription of the trial proper began. A day or so later, on another visit, I discovered that what I had assumed to be another copy of the same book (this one in a different, finer binding) was in fact a first edition, published in 1910, the year after the first trial. I read the obviously substantially different long introduction to this volume too, (I had, by the way, read treatments of the Slater case before) in which it was already quite obvious that the author, William Roughead, felt the Guilty verdict to be utterly unwarranted, although, of course, he could not say so in quite so many words. Little good this (widespread) belief did Slater for nearly 20 years. ("It is not too much to say that the verdict came with a shock of surprise to most of the auditors in the crowded courtroom," Roughead remarks, though perhaps elsewhere, for my own chaotic notes do not mention the provenance of the quotation. (Is it not a reasonable rule of thumb that, where the accused is found guilty of murder to the general surprise of the court, something is amiss? All the same, I accept that one could hardly build a legal tradition on this.))

I have made one further visit to the shelf since then (yesterday, Saturday, in fact) where I began the unsystematic reading of the actual witnesses' evidence (Barrowman's Mother, Barrowman herself, Trench, Adams, Lambie, and a P.C. McNeil), and I expect over the near future to read the entire transcript as opportunity presents itself, and concentration allows. (A major shock yesterday "Q: "Had you heard that old Miss Gilchrist was a resetter?"—"TRENCH: "I have heard that frequently." (A —resetter— is the Scottish legal term for a—fence—, a person who —recycles— stolen property then puts it back into circulation at a profit. I also learned yesterday, for the first time, that Miss Gilchrist kept a dog which had died 3 months before her own fateful night, and which she was convinced had been poisoned. A suggestion was made (I do not know with what justice) that what we had here was the deliberate removal of a guard-dog.))

It is curious to put back on a shelf a volume dealing with an old murder and then to walk back home past many of the major locations of the crime. (The more so if one happens to meet almost at once, as I did yesterday, someone one knows, with whom one stops to chat full in the sight of the building where Slater was staying on the night of the murder, and out of whose windows he must so often have glanced.

(Before I go on, I should mention the possibility that occurs to me, in conjunction with my earlier suggestion that the killer may have visited the library; that his reason for this, as good a reason as any one might think, could have been to consult the transcript of the trial, and perhaps to grimace with ill-concealed mirth, or relief, or fear at the sight of some detail lying undisturbed before him of the implications of which only he was fully aware. (I note that someone has made a few light pencil marks at some time in the last 75 years ("Acquired 22 April 1910"), but, whoever it was, it was probably not the murderer. (At one point during the Lord Advocate's speech, when that gentleman is explaining why this careful, scientific thief stole only one item of jewelry where hundreds were lying about unattended, our unknown annotator loses his temper, misreads the point being made and notes "a lie", instead of the more accurate (having, I think, underlined in reference the phrase "more than one item of jewelry") "a long shot" (but perhaps I misrepresent him, for I merely noticed this in passing.))))

The more so if this man, on finding out what I have just been doing, should at once tell me of the street in Ayr where Slater died; that he used to deliver a newspaper (another newspaper!) to the perfectly ordinary bungalow next door to Slater's own perfectly ordinary 1930's bungalow (with, he claims, only a little gallows on the gatepost for identification) and that he was always obscurely worried, being a mere youth, that Slater might run out and poison him. The conversation then drifted on to other things. (Such as the 1927 Condon-Lonnigan Chicagoans' version of "Nobody's Sweetheart", with the very young Gene Krupa's astonishing display of rhythmically alert drumming, carried out probably while Slater (who was not released until November the 14th of that year) was still in custody. (Slater was in jail long enough for an entire new art form, jazz, to develop and reach its peak in the other world. (And silent films

28

too. Slater was in prison surely for almost all the life-time of the silent film (not entirely inappropriate given his own long out-of-sight silence) with all the crowds, hysteria, new buildings, and sociological re-orientation that that involved.))))

Having learned the exact number of the house in St. George's Road where Slater stayed for two months, I took care to note it as I passed, and I was surprised to find that it was quite different from the one which I had hitherto rather carelessly always assumed to be the house in question. Thus it was not the first close round the corner from West Princes Street, where a childhood friend of mine used to stay (curiously enough, also called Grant, the same name as the next street up, on the right), but it lay some way beyond—indeed it was the very last doorway before the eventual intersection with Woodlands Road. This is part of a very fine red sandstone tenement building, highly characterized, with turreted windows, tiny balconies, and much intricate detail besides. Two long facades sweep down towards an acute-angled intersection but do not quite meet. A third, short but vital facade separates them, above the entrance-way to Stuart and Stuart's furniture shop, which entirely occupies that brief pavement. (I bought the modest carpet-squares which help decorate the floor of my room in here a few years ago. (Slater furnished his flat with furniture from this store too, then also known as Stuart and Stuart's. *(In 1986, after I had finished writing this work, this landmark incredibly changed its title, having (I suppose) been taken over by someone else.)))* This facade has so impressed me that I once had a very vivid dream of living behind it. I also, in a novel I once wrote, based a moderately prominent building on this one. I can put my hand on my heart and say quite honestly that I have often walked past underneath it, gazing upwards, and thinking, what a superb place to live that must be, except perhaps that, with the new motorway being so near it now, it must be terribly noisy. Of course, I am still not utterly certain that Slater lived behind any of that part of the facade, for I have never gone up the close stairway, and it may be there is more than one flat on each landing, and Slater's might have been full over St. George's Road. Nor have I ever, as far as I recall, climbed the stairway of Miss Gilchrist's close, even though I lived right at the top of the next stairway and climbed and descended it many thousands of times. (I intend to do so soon.) It was strange to walk by identifying doors and windows. (Until a few days ago, I had always assumed that the murder took place in what had in fact been the empty flat above.) The actual windows are now ribbed and opaque, and seem to be devoted to some sort of manufacturer of dental equipment. But the next stairway along (No. 61—almost opposite Queen's Crescent) I have climbed more than once. For, a year or so ago, I made the acquaintance of someone who has a room in the top-floor flat there, which I have visited a few times, and who, to the best of my knowledge, still lives there.

Eight

Another thing which I discovered, accidentally, on the open shelves of that library room were a complete set of Post Office Directories for the city (including lists of the inhabitants of the houses of each street) dating back until before 1850. I at once reached for the 1909 volume, and, yes, there they were. An A.P. Adams at No. 61, a Miss Gilchrist (in those very words) at No. 49 next door. I ran my eyes quickly down the list of inhabitants of No. 37, the close where I was born, hoping to memorize the names of these silent neighbours (needless to say I did not manage this) who, to my recollection, are not mentioned anywhere in the trial. I then plucked out the next volume, located the appropriate column, and glanced down. All was substantially as before, but to the alert eye there was a gap between No. 61 and No. 49; the absence of Miss Gilchrist had completely removed the house she lived in. (Evidently the flat above was still empty. (A quick look at the 1908 volume showed the reverend gentleman still comfortably installed here. Everyone was already quietly settled in the street. (Doubtless people were coming and going elsewhere in the thoroughfare: I did not examine it at length. To a cursory glance, all the immediate inhabitants seemed to be the same. (Curious that I must have relatives, on my mother's side, scattered throughout the book, and yet I do not at present know enough to find them. (Is the murderer's name included? Very possibly. (And is it also in previous and subsequent editions? Who knows for certain that it isn't?))))))

Truly, the contents of these volumes are so immense as to be beyond writing about. One could trace an endless pattern of windings in and out, of comings and goings, and, perhaps even more impressive, of people living in the same house for 30 or 40 years, and then suddenly disappearing for no good reason. I imagine these misleadingly grim-looking volumes will draw me back time and again. (I had already acquired one of my own—bought a while back at a secondhand bookshop. It dated from the early 1960's, and includes the name "Mrs. Kuppner" first on the list of occupants of No. 37. (Perhaps my father was hiding in a cupboard when the gentleman, if gentleman it was, making the list called). I can see it from where I sit, and could go across and discover who was then occupying the Gilchrist flat, but it is resting beneath such a huge pile of precariously balanced books that it is probably safer just to let it be. (I did take out at the time, if I remember rightly, the 1951 volume—the year of my birth—and my father's name was there proclaimed quite unequivocally. (I wonder now if any name in the street was the same as it had been 42 years before.) The murderous address again boasted two occupants. (I then checked the address at which I at present live—now barbarously broken down into individual rented rooms—and found that a Mrs. Lightbody had been in occupance here at the time of my birth. (Intrigued, I took out the last volume in the sequence—some years old, but I was already here then—and discovered a name, attached to my present address, which I never once encountered before. I still do not understand the meaning of this.)))

Nine

One of the local architectural books which I bought some weeks ago contains, as a bonus, a fascinating partial reproduction of a Glasgow map of 1866, centred on Charles Wilson's Park Circus area. This comfortably includes the relevant streets, and shows that, at that date, West Princes Street did not stretch further west than Ashley Street (the first intersection on its long south side—then called (as it still was at the trial) West Cumberland Street). This explains why the length of the south facade facing Queen's Crescent was given the name Queen's Terrace; for in the layout of those days, West Princes Street could be read as merely an introduction, opening onto an architecturally distinct crescent feature. However, as West Princes Street commenced its march westwards, beyond the crescent, Queen's Terrace became very obviously nothing more than a part of the southern aspect of the street with a peculiarly favoured view, and was renumbered in accordance with the roadway which had absorbed it, even though the indigenes apparently clung to the older, perhaps more select designation, thereby causing a certain amount of confusion. (Nobody calls it Queen's Terrace nowadays. (Although, I remember I did once receive a most welcome letter from someone whose address was both a high number of Sauchiehall Street, and a low number of Fitzroy Place—so that apparently in Sauchiehall Street (the buildings are on the 1866 map) the process was never quite consummated)).

Curiously enough, if I turn over four pages back from the map, we reach a photograph of precisely the introductory piece of West Princes Street, and are instructed that this section was already a quarter of a century old by 1866, even though any continuation was yet to come. (We see principally the opposite side of the street, including the windows cut across by the climbing stairway, from which Miss Gilchrist's house could have been observed. Someone is walking down the foreshortened near side at a point in between Miss Gilchrist's door, and the entrance to the close where we used to live.)

But all I really wished to say (Slater's house is not yet built) is that, on perusing the map, I noticed the name India Street on what is today the northern continuation of Elderslie Street (although, actually, in this instance I sympathise with the earlier fractiousness: this part even nowadays does not *feel* as if it is still Elderslie Street). This

33

led me to suspect that my earlier ruminations on events taking place in that street might have been modestly misplaced. Perhaps they indeed were. However, on checking the modern location of *my* India Street, I discover that, yes, there was indeed another one already in loco . And as there seem to be many more houses in this one, it still seems the likelier possibility. *(My fears were groundless. The first India Street was indeed the one in question.)*

(Blythswood Square is on the extreme right of the map, but the Madeleine Smith affair was almost ten years old by now. Sandyford Place—part of Sauchiehall Street (actually, it continues Fitzroy Place on the other side of Elderslie Street)—which was the venue of the M'Lachlan debacle (in which the chief prosecution witness was instrumental in the conviction of the female accused for a murder which he himself committed)—is plumb in the middle of the page. But that was four years ago. (How *well-behaved* the map looks nonetheless). Last year, 1865, was that of Pritchard the poisoner, and perhaps his house in Sauchiehall Street, of whose location I am not absolutely certain, just creeps onto the right-hand edge of the street-plan. This was, at that time, the newer, fashionable part of the city.)

Ten

Another curious coincidence has cropped up. I was sitting, on a Monday afternoon, at a large desk in the library, half-way through reading the verbatim account of the Lord Advocate's rather disgraceful performance, through which an irate reader has picked (probably) his way apparently a very long time ago, placing little question-marks and underlinings at the, to him, most insupportable lapses and injustices. (I think I now understand better the reason for the annotation "a lie" beside the learned advocate's remark that Slater was disturbed in his orgy of theft after laying his hands on only one item. For, of course, quite apart from the fact that he was never there, the stolen item of jewelry—if there was one—was not the subject of any attempt by the prosecution to link it to Slater (wisely enough, one might think), and they thus cannot now, as it were, palm it off on him by a sleight of hand. (Brilliantly done though, eh? Fiat justitia.)

Anyway, while I was doing so, a voice suddenly broke in upon me from the left, and a youngish man of roughly my age apologetically remarked that he had noticed while passing by that I was reading about Oscar Slater (I had been investigating a photograph thereabouts, I think) and that I was taking notes. A few hastily exchanged sentences bore witness to a shared obsession, and, ten minutes later, we were sitting in the ground-floor cafe of the library, and he (who obviously knows far more about it than I do) was giving me my first insight into some of the subtler points or implications of the case. It is possible that I have been distinctly naive in accepting the generally current version of events quite so uncritically. He seems, perhaps through deeper knowledge, to be more sympathetic towards the predicament of the powers-that-be than I am. Certainly, my own rather uncritically gathered and rather simple-minded view that the man who walked past Lambie and Adams was an estranged member of the family, whom Lambie recognised and identified, and who was either the murderer or an associate—(the sole live question with regard to the behaviour of the police being: were their actions entirely the result of incompetence, or was there something more sinister at work?)—is left looking a little superficial. He seemed to believe that this man was indeed the murderer, but that Lambie mistook him for someone else, and identified him as such to Miss Birrell. This does raise the fascinating possibility that the police never even got to within touching distance of the murderer, but, inevitably, it raises new problems. (Chief among them being: what right did the police have to attempt to hide this turn of events by evasions, lies and admonitions to Lambie not to repeat what she said immediately after the murder during that precipitous flight of hers to Miss Gilchrist's niece. I believe this is known as doctoring the evidence, not to say some sort of fraud, and, according to certain authorities, is even reckoned to be illegal. But my thus accidentally acquired fellow-sufferer, who is, I think, a journalist, possesses six books of newspaper clippings relating to the case, and he fielded all the questions I threw at him with the calm assurance of an expert, so we exchanged addresses and phone-numbers, and it could be that I have found an extremely valuable new source. We shall see.

(Apparently there is no chance whatsoever that Miss Gilchrist was herself in any way criminal. This, it seems, is a lurid fantasy which must be given up. Evidently theories were current in Glasgow just after her murder that she was Slater's mother; that she was Lambie's mother; and so on. The theory that she was the mother of *both* of them would spring irresistably to the Jacobean mind. (The daughter of an ex-servant of hers bore the name Marion Gilchrist Ferguson. A new will, codiciled the month before she died, left the bulk of her money to this woman and her daughter. (Who presumably inherited. The point is—it was specifically denied, in largest part, to kith and kin. Which is interesting.))) (By the way, it is being more and more borne in upon me that the man who appeared at Kelvinbridge Underground Station and would not wait for a ticket had nothing whatever to do with this. He was probably only one more man in a hurry. (Though I should be rather sorry to see him go, and cannot give him up quite so easily.))

(Before I forget, I should unequivocally add that, for all the exciting shock of the pleasant new vistas opened up by the question put at the trial about Miss Gilchrist's possibly being a receiver of stolen goods, it is as certain as anything can be in this case—I think I have remarked before that at times it seems that the only thing certainly known about this case is that Slater was not the murderer—that she came by the jewels perfectly lawfully. A representative of (I forget exactly the circumstances) a wholesale jeweller gave evidence of receipts of numerous transactions involving uncut stones. (A strange hobby for an old woman, perhaps. But who knows what the hobbies of her neighbours were?) In short, Miss Gilchrist was definitely not on nodding terms with the criminal fraternity.

(I should also say that I have done Madeleine Smith a disservice. Yesterday evening, on arriving home, after spending much time at the library reading the two volumes which seem to be just about all the secondary literature that exists on *her* case (in the margin of one

36

of which, strangely enough, someone has penned, in tiny tiny blue letters, the name which, until yesterday, successfully sheltered from me behind the letters A.B. (the man identified by Lambie in the *Slater* case)) I picked up my copy of her trial-book ("Famous Scottish Trials: Madeleine Smith"—published in 1905; which is to say, during Miss Gilchrist's lifetime (and indeed, during that of Smith herself, come to that)), finished reading the interminable love-letters which had bored me off the volume at my previous attempt to read it, and discovered, on glancing at the introduction, that the voting on her case had been 13 to 2 for Not Proven over Guilty, and not 10 to 5. This rather worries me, inasmuch as I was so serenely certain that it had been the narrower verdict.))

Eleven

Although no doubt it does not look like it, a few weeks have intervened since last I wrote any part of this work (long enough, I imagine, to travel to and back from America in an ocean liner), while I have been busy with other things. When I return to them, however, I find that, rather eerily, the books of the trial, the photographs etc., are all impressively unaltered, except doubtless for mild rearrangements on a more or less molecular level. I am also unsure about what I have already written, and, indeed, uncertain as to the whereabouts of those former doodlings of mine on this subject, which are now, I suppose, deeply involved in the general untidiness of my room. They may quite possibly be permanently lost, of course; and, if so, it is a loss which legal history will, I imagine, manage to come to terms with without undue heartsearchings or loss of sleep; but I am loth to recommence my modest labours on that depressing assumption, and will therefore suppose that they are out there somewhere, and will eventually return to light.

When I began writing this, I was, I suppose, a naive follower of the common-sense view. On this reading, Slater's case is remarkable not only in that an innocent man served nearly 20 years in prison for a murder he did not commit (which is completely true), but also for the fact that the murderer (or one of the murderers, (or the associate of the murderer (in fact, probably THE MURDERER))) coolly walked out of the house straight past two eye-witnesses. This is true too. But the common-sense view also involves the belief that Lambie, one of these witnesses (the other was a short-sighted man, caught on the hop without his glasses) instantly recognised the man from previous visits as a distant relative of the deceased, and ran almost at once to a nearby niece of Miss Gilchrist, where she graphically reported what she thought she had just seen. This also, I still believe, is true. Needless to say, on this view, Lambie is right. The murderer is the man she identified (famously disguised, in the 1914 enquiry, as A.B.), and the mystery is, why in God's name did the police not arrest him, have him committed to trial , and sit back, comfortable in the knowledge of a job well done? (Or why, if A.B. had an alibi, or could otherwise be dimissed from the list of plausible suspects, were they not open about this; which would, at the least, have surely saved a good deal of trouble to all and sundry?)

I have, however, by now had a couple of subsequent discussions with the man I met at the Mitchell Library (whom, following the fashion set by the case, I shall therefore nominate as M.L.)—a journalist who is obviously immersed up to his ears in the facts of this case—and he is convinced that (to almost echo a contemporary locution of the police hierarchy) A.B. had nothing whatever to do with it. He further claims to have (and I am almost certain that he does in fact have) further evidence which he will not divulge to me, which, although unsensational, makes it even more unlikely to him that A.B. is the man in question.

It should be noted that A.B. was a man of (I am told) 33, who was familiar with the interior of Miss Gilchrist's house; who was positively identified by an eye-witness who already knew him; who lived ten minutes' walk away; and whose alibi (as far as I can gather, but this may be quite wrong) was that he was sitting innocently at home on his own (just like Slater) while all this was going on. This is, on any reading, highly suggestive. Despite any subsequent bizarreness to their behaviour, if we assume, as I do, that Trench was telling the truth (I fail to see how anyone can do otherwise—but no doubt this is a tribute my the narrowness of my imagination), and that Lambie's mentioning of A.B. was known to the police, who, of course, would investigate him anyway as a matter of course, we can hardly doubt that the shrieking suspiciousness of all this was as evident to them as to us, and ask what motive they could have had in scoring A.B. off their list, other than extremely strong, indeed overwhelming, evidence to the contrary, which was not made public. I am at a loss to suggest such a motive, but I must say that the subsequent behaviour of this collection of less than sublime policemen, particularly vis-a-vis Trench and Cook, whom it seems fair to me to say they hounded to an early grave, was such that I don't know that we can safely assume that no such motive existed. (Did they simply get it quickly into their heads that Slater must have done it, and reshape the entire spatio-temporal universe inside and outside their heads accordingly? I wish I knew. But I certainly don't see why they should be given the benefit of the doubt.)

Twelve

I suppose I may as well set down now what I think of the case, for what it's worth, which isn't much. It seems to me still that there is practically nothing one can be sure about, except that Slater did not do it. Was there one man or two involved? (To go no further.) Arguing for two, we have Agnes Brown, who, if she is to be believed, saw two men running down West Princes Street, to disappear into Rupert Street, slightly before twelve minutes past seven. This is distinctly impressive. We have it agreed on all sides that West Princes Street was a very quiet street. And presumably the escaper did not stop running as soon as he reached the foot of the stairs. Of course, this pair could have been two quite different men. The universe could end in two minutes time. Sooner or later we will have to prefer something, unless we are to conclude that, really, the old woman was not killed at all.

But it is undeniable that two men running down a street, even if in flight from the scene of a murder, does not necessarily argue two men inside Miss Gilchrist's house. One of them could, for whatever reason, have been waiting outside. (At around that time, if the witnesses are to be believed to any degree, West Princes Street also seems to have been a popular place to wait in.) Which leaves us with the absence of any blood on the match and matchbox, and the absence of blood on the man leaving the scene of the crime—or, at least, leaving an almost adjacent bedroom. Well, he could have been wearing gloves. He could have put on his coat subsequent to the attack. And, of course, there is the famous (and utterly convincing) theory of the manner of the killing. Several repetitive downward thrusts to the head of a figure lying on the floor, administered via the rear leg of a heavy wooden chair—with the chair shielding the assailant from most of the escaping blood. (Detectives walked all round this chair, failing to find a murder weapon.) I must say, if anything like this happened, it seems to me to be rather more likely that the person who did it was on his own (apart from the victim), rather than in company. Although, of course, one never knows.

As for the fact that the (let us presume) single murderer at once went into the spare bedroom, lit the gas with a single match, forgot about the matchbox ((!)—a matchbox, apparently not of any of the usual household brands, was indeed helpfully left behind), and straightaway busied himself with Miss Gilchrist's locked document-box, what are we to make of this? Was the sought-for document (if there was one) always incriminating, or did it merely become so in the light of subsequent (unforeseen) developments? If the former holds, then it was scarcely necessary to kill the old woman to obtain the document, particularly if one was alone in the house with her and one also knew where it was secreted. (Of course, he could have begun to go and get it anyway, have shoved her aside, protesting; have accidentally caused her to fall; and so on.) Such a document would have to be fairly shattering in its implications—in which case what could it possibly be? Are we somehow to assume that Miss Gilchrist was a blackmailer? If so, (I don't believe it for a moment), it was the best-kept secret of a trial rife with unfounded rumours. And besides, the old lady had, at the very least, a safe in her parlour for her more valuable mementoes.

I am slightly troubled by the reticence of commentators to enlighten the struggler after truth as to the nature of exactly what was normally kept in this box. Documents were scattered over the floor, cursorily scanned and rejected (literacy is a great thing), and I assume they were the minutiae of everyday life, bills and receipts and suchlike, too insignificant to talk about. If the murderer's pet was among them—and he obviously knew it to be so (or at least that it *ought* to be so)—then presumably it was of equal putative unimportance. Yet, setting aside the possibility of an absentminded-ness of legendary proportions, this inoffensive piece of (presumably) paper was of literally life and death importance to him.

Sir Arthur Conan Doyle, I believe, suggested a will. Can this poss-ibly be right? Unless the assailant already possessed all other copies of the will (which points to a lawyer as the guilty party), what use would a single copy be (a hand-written draft of a new one?), and, anyway, what could a will say that was actually *incriminating?* (One would hardly hang around on the scene of such a crime merely to eliminate a copy of a will which one found to be, well, financially unfortunate. Or would one?) And, besides: the will would surely be in the safe? I, of course, do not know what the sought document was (perhaps it was never there; perhaps it was there and no-one read it and realised its significance (perhaps the murderer was, in effect, putting himself to a lot of worry for nothing)), but I am proud of the fact that I managed to work out a theoretical shape for it which is at least consistent with the facts, though almost certainly inaccurate. The murderer (who, of course, at that time was only an acquaintance) wrote to the old lady telling her when he next (I favour, *next*) intended to visit her; and she kept this not very important letter among her not very important papers. Or she threw it away as trivial, but the man did not know this, and so had to search for it in its likeliest location anyway, just in case. True, this argues for considerable presence of mind on the killer's part (if killer it was), but, although we may not know the man's identity, we do know, particularly from the suave manner of his exit, that presence of mind was a quality which he certainly possessed in abundance.

Thirteen

Yesterday evening, I went to have a look at the house which, on my latest information, was occupied by the mysterious A.B. at the time of the killing. When I say "went to look at it", I perhaps risk giving the misleading impression that I had to go out of my way to see it. In fact it is a large house on the main road slightly in towards the city centre from the west of the city where I stay, and I have passed it literally thousands of times. Indeed, I am quite certain that I have more than once scrutinised it closely as I passed. It stands directly next to the famously slender-spired Landsdowne Church of John Honeyman (which I have on several occasions admired from a Chinese restaurant directly opposite (I would go there much more often if their cheap midday menu included the offer of Chinese rather than Western soup)) and it has thus more than once, as it were, inherited the architectural stare which that other building wrings from me. Certainly the official sign now on the door came as no startling revelation to me. I find that it is almost directly opposite the site of Kelvinside Underground Station, into which someone possibly raced just over half an hour after the murder. As a man could run thither in less than ten minutes, and limp in less than twenty, there is an obvious discrepancy here. I thus tremblingly point out the possibility that the murderer, or whoever, might have had occasion to visit a house in the locality for quarter of an hour or so. Indeed, if two people were involved, some consultation in safe surroundings would perhaps have been thought advisable before they split up, quite apart from welcoming the opportunity to wash hands, throw up, or whatever. Of course, returning to the open air would be a traumatic experience, and one might wish to keep human contact to the minimum—though one would not want to go on a long walk either. However, the coin-flinger may never have existed, or, if he did, have had nothing at all to do with the small group of people now already forming and reforming around that particular nearby dead body.

All the same, I have had other reasons for observing this house. It is the front-door house of a tenement. Next to it comes another doorway, to the upper floors of the building, and then the five lateral windows of another ground-floor house, whose door is round the corner, in a pleasant terrace. The first two of these windows are discreetly lettered with a dentist's name, and the last two with the

43

name of his partner. This first dentist is the one which I go to, and have gone to for years. (Actually, I had a postcard from there three or four weeks ago, telling me it was time for another check-up, which I am at present studiously ignoring.) The celebrated door is thus the second last such item I see before I enter my dentists's hallway. I have, thus, more than once gazed at it longingly, on my way to an appointment with pain, somewhat hurt by its indifference and tantalized by its air of security.

I remember now that, that afternoon, I was stopped by a young woman in nearby Woodlands Road, and asked directions to the street which happens to house my dentist.

I have only ever visited two dentists. The earlier of them—a man I still harbour a considerable grudge against—had a surgery a few blocks away, also entered by the first door in a sidestreet; the windows also giving a view of the main road, and another famous church, this time by G. G. Scott. I mention this chiefly because this street, known as Woodlands Drive nowadays, was once, I think, called Blythswood Terrace, and it is where Miss Gilchrist's Miss Birrell was living on the night of the murder, when Helen Lambie ran to inform her of what she thought had just happened. On one view, A.B.'s house contained a man sitting or standing, reading innocently, or, at any rate, doing nothing suspicious. On another view, God knows what was happening. This Miss Birrell soon moved, to a street 15 minutes' walk away, past the Underground Station, known then, I think, as Kelvinside Terrace, and now known as Wilton Street. I live in Wilton Street at present. In fact, I am sitting writing at a bay window, from which I could, if I wished, look out at her very house, but that would be pointless, would it not?

I should, of course, add that Slater, when he took up his residence in St. George's Road, put a sign on the door which said, "A. Anderson, Dentist". I fear I am approaching the point at which I begin to believe that I have dreamed up this entire case.

Fourteen

Also, a couple of days ago, I climbed the stairs to the door of Miss Gilchrist's house. The outside door, the close-door, is nowadays permanently open. There is no more of this unlocking it from inside by means of a lever, which we heard of at the trial. (Of course, the newly renovated tenements of the area have a sort of electronic substitute for this procedure, whereby the visitor identifies himself on an intercom before being let in to the building. (I well remember the relics of the old system still visible on each landing of the house where I lived as a child. On the back wall equidistant from the two doors of the houses facing each other was a curiously shaped brass object, comprising a rectangular piece which was much taller than broad with a vertical slit up and down which one could sterilely manipulate a protruding knobbed handle. This sounds like a particularly obscene symbolic activity, but there was no fun in it whatever. It was all so obviously pointless. More than once, we enquired of a parent what its purpose was, and received answers the accuracy of which I am no longer able to gauge. But many is the time when, on one of those occasions when I returned home as a schoolboy, and everyone was mysteriously out (it is curious how deep a mark standing at an unattended door for twenty minutes or so etches into the memory) I would, desperately inventing ways of passing the time, noisily pull the small lever up and down until I had wrought myself to a sensational public climax and the applause—no, and again peer over the banister, perhaps drawn by that utterly magical sound, hidden footsteps far below which are almost certainly those of one's mother. (Rather than those of a returning young female servant.)))
There were surprisingly few stairs—three flights of eight each, rather shallow, as I remember. One could hurry down them in five seconds. They are so old and chipped and worn that they are obviously the original stonework. For the rest, however, all is changed. A completely modern, glassless door, painted a startling blue, and unencumbered by signs (obviously part of the industrial firm from next door) has replaced the original. It is, however, surprisingly narrow. The man leaving must have brushed right up against Adams as he did so, before haring away down the stairs. Certainly, Lambie's revised evidence, that she too was at the door when the man walked past, is not given any more plausibility (of which it is in great need) by the constrictedness of the entrance. I also glanced up at the turning

stair leading to the upper floor, untenanted in December 1909, but, on observing that to climb there would take me too ostentatiously past a window clearly visible from the street, I decided not to go up. I must say though, that I did feel a moment of psychological certainty that no-one, escaping from the scene of a murder would have hurried up those stairs rather than down. The whole place felt so small and somehow encaged. (I do not found this feeling, m'lud, on the transparency of the windows.)

There was little cause for me to remain there, and so I descended at once, at normal pace. My still wet footprints going down met the wetter prints of my arrival. So now my footprints too have stained that stairway. (The footprints, by the way, are a rather interesting point. Lambie said that, on her return with the newspaper, she noticed two wet footprints on the inner stairway, at the base. According to the evidence of the policeman on that beat, "When I passed at 10 minutes to 7, rain was falling." As far as I recall, he went to get his cape shortly afterwards. It seems likely to me that the footprints were Adams's, who needed scarcely get his shoes wet in going from one doorway to the other. Failing that, they were the visitor's very first steps inside that building, the remainder of whose wet steps had presumably dried out by then. That someone else took a step in through the open door, hesitated, then left, is, however, an image nice enough for us mention it, no matter what we might think of its plausibility.)

I may as well, metaphorically of course, drift sideways at this point, and consider whether I myself have ever climbed those steps before. I am not aware of having done so, but I am very much aware of having been a child who lived on the next stairway, and who habitually played outside in the warmer weather, with other local children, games which frequently involved hiding at convenient points in the available architecture. It would assuredly be some sort of statistical miracle if I had never once, perhaps during a game of hide and seek, (how many thousands of such moments disappear, completely unremembered, until perhaps some other children are heard, with devastating sudden clarity, playing in an identical style somewhere just beyond this new window whose very existence was wholly unknown during all those games of one's own)—if I had never once climbed those historic stairs, more or less half a century after the fact. Such is life, as Ned Kelly, the legendary Australian bandit, remarked on the scaffold. (There are certainly photographs of these buildings extant in Australia—or there certainly were until recently, for I clearly remember our family standing beside a car at the tip of Queen's Crescent, with the famous buildings in the background (although ours is the one they were trying to preserve), for the benefit of some visiting Australian relatives. (My favourite famous last words, by the way, are Lady Mary Wortley Montague's, "It has all been very interesting". ("Montague", even more by the way, was the witness Arthur Adams's middle name. (Montague St. is the last turning to the left or right off West Princes Street before it meets Park Road in the west.)) (It might perhaps not be wholly idle to speculate as to what Miss Gilchrist's last words might have been. Did they in some way provoke an attack, catching her (perhaps all too literally) off balance? ("I have given you all the money/help I am ever going to give you." "Give me one good reason why I should change my mind." "I know perfectly well you would never dare to, Frank." "NO; I will not tell you where they are.") There is, as far as I can see, no way whatever of knowing this. Even the more flagrant inventions, ("Oh, hit me again, inspector, you know how much I love it",) are dismissed with a minuscule but real hesitancy.))

I can, however, clearly remember more than once going up to the door which is just inside the close, on the left of the first stairway. This led to the flight of steps down to the back garden. It was almost invariably locked. As such, it was a route we had recourse to, once its reputation as a no-through-road was established, only in cases of emergency, when all else had failed. This back garden was immediately contiguous with our own, but, unlike our neighbour on the left, where the ground continued at the same level, and which could easily be entered by either of two institutionalised gaps in the intervening fencing, this one was distinctly foreign territory. Not only was the ground away down on a markedly lower level than ours, and separated by a large stone wall which, though fairly low at the uphill end, consolidated itself into an impresssively high barrier by the time it reached the rear of the houses; but it differed from our two in extent as well. It reached much further back, towards a brick wall by a lane, round the side of the monolithic rear of a large garage in neighbouring Grant Street, which, although it nicked a corner from the other garden's more privileged rectangle, was utterly callous with us, hemming us in badly along its entire extent.

Needless to say, if any of the games we played involved a rubber ball—and they usually did—this ball sooner or later would find itself taking an unlucky bounce and disappearing over the said wall. This was not in itself an insoluble problem, for that obstruction, at its more modest extremity, was easily scalable. Nonetheless, there were quite a few possible complicating factors to be taken into account. The herbage of the lower garden was thick—grass and weeds—and extensive, and contained many areas which a small ball could hide itself in, if its progress had not been observed. And even if one of us had managed to watch it bounce or trundle towards its unsolicited goal, we could frequently do no more than direct our attention towards the area of its last known sighting, and assume it had not taken too flagrant an invisible bounce or deflection. But, actually, as I remember, rooting around among weed stems, grasses, and varieties of fragmented brick, was quite a pleasant occupation, provided it could be conducted free of mental stress. Unfortunately, there was in the tenement overlooking that back garden an old man (and, I think I remember, an old woman too) whose main pastime in retirement seemed to be flinging up a window noisily and shouting at children who were breaching their wall-lined privacy to get back where they came from. This happened so often that it definitely became the norm, and so, even on those occasions when we sucessfully penetrated to that part of the garden which we thought the most likely resting place of our recently liberated cheap rubber spheroid, we could never be entirely sure, however discreetly we searched, that nemesis was not just about to snap into life and shoo us off. (This did happen more than once. With what ridiculous haste we raced away. Actually, we were in far more danger of injuring ourselves on such a precipitate retreat back over the wall than we had ever been on our stealthy, careful previous advance.)

I remember those engrossing hunts through an undergrowth magnified by loss. Occasionally we would find caterpillars on the broader leaves of the bordering pansies, and we gazed absorbed at these sensationally complex little beasts, which almost seem to have been designed specifically to enchant children. Sometimes we failed to find the ball; sometimes we found it at once, with suspicious speed, as if *someone else* were helpfully drawing its unlikely position to our attention; sometimes we discovered it in a desperate investigation, far away, impossibly far away, from where, by any of the normal laws of terrestrial physics, it ought to have been. Occasionally we would triumphantly find a ball which had been lost on a previous date, just on the humdrum side of legend (how disconsolate it looked—an abandoned infant, totally passive, which had neither grown, nor changed, nor cried), and we would have to decide whether to take what we now had, and run (which, if the new ball were a better one, we would probably soon do, with triumphant, self-congratulatory cries of, "It's just as well we lost the old one, isn't it!"); or carry on our search for the one we had so recently misplaced. And, of course, sometimes we would find a ball which no-one recognised. These we looked on almost as a direct statement of Providential favour; a sign that the universe was, basically, good. Either one of us had lost it so long ago that its memory was no longer recoverable (a few months in childhood, I suppose); or it had been there for longer than our games had been going on beside it.

(Presumably a ball might lie there for years unmolested, as their owners grew up into perfect imitation adults. (Or had they been lost there by other children? What other children? We never saw other children in that garden, whether playing or searching. It was, except for our own brief raiding parties, a childless garden. We seemed to be the only children who even knew that that garden existed.))

I find it slightly curious to consider that this was, presumably, the same back garden that the police looked through carefully, so long before, searching for a murder weapon. (A typically brilliant performance, considering that the weapon was, in all probability, a large mahogany chair which they had to walk round in order to examine the body.) An auger was found, with a few grey hairs adhering to it. But this had been there for a long while, unnoticed, and it was dismissed as not being relevant to the case. (Too bad for whoever the grey hairs belonged to. (What might one not have found, slumbering untroubled in other back-gardens in 1908 Glasgow? (Or anywhere else, for that matter.) Another fascinating, unrecorded collection. After all, this is human history too.))

I try to see more clearly in my mind's eye the windows which the old man leaned out of. For a moment I was lit up by the idea that this might have been the same man, Arthur. M. Adams, who saw the murderer, who testified in the case, but the fact he died in 1942 (albeit while still inhabiting the same house—one would not have been surprised had he moved, following the murder (but who would buy?)) is, alas, pretty seriously prejudicial to this dazzling theory. He shouted from a low window, but not from the lowest; and I cannot for the life of me see how I can avoid the conclusion that, although it cannot have been Adams himself (perhaps it was Adams' ghost?) it was someone shouting at us from Adams' house. (It might have been the murderer, of course, but one would need more information on the matter to be quite sure. (A joke. (I think.)))

It got to the stage that a high wooden frame (filled by netted wire) was added to the partitioning wall, to dissuade us youth from paying our unwelcome visits. Needless to say, it did nothing of the sort; particularly as clambering over the obstruction had something of the exhilaration of climbing the swaying rigging of a sailing ship. However, it did slow us up, and gave rise to a greater level of incidental noise, all of which increased our own Watcher's opportunities of catching us in the act.

Normally, being warned off would be the end of it. But there were times, particularly if we could actually see the ball lying there, in full view, agonisingly recoverable, perhaps on the path, or right up against a wall, and when a lightning raid would clearly reclaim it, that we decided on the last resort, that of going round to the door

I have mentioned, in the main street, to the left of the stairway. (By the way, I do not recall ever seeing this door to the back garden talked of in the literature. I presume it was kept firmly locked even then. But it would be worth saying so explicitly, for, if it wasn't, then the murderer had a choice of entrances or exits. But surely it must have been locked.) In the normal run of things, we would try the handle, and instantly discover the futility of our hopes. However, miraculously, two or three times, THE DOOR OPENED, and we stepped timorously through into the lost world.

We could tell it was a lost world, and not just a neighbouring state, because this arrangement was utterly different from our own, or from that in our neighbouring close to the left. In these, the stairway to the back was through a gate on the right hand side of the main tenement stairway. If pulled shut, it locked itself automatically, but it was still possible to bypass it by climbing onto the curving banister rail beside it, which continued unbroken down towards the lower level. In doing so, one momentarily risked death by falling to the basement underneath, but it was a sort of unwritten rule of close life that no-one would ever be allowed to die or be injured in such a way, and we had quite astonishing confidence that this law would always be respected.

Of the dark, musty, irregular-cornered basements at the foot of the stairway, I have many memories. We would shelter there during sharp showers, or when hiding from any inconvenient adult or child who was searching for us. I still remember the abruptness with which, not in our basement, or the one on the left, but in the one to the left of that—the last, or more properly, the first, in our street, (this was a curious retreat in the inside turn of the corner of St. George's Road, (a main thoroughfare which is now half obliterated))—the girl that I was hiding with, who I was not particularly known to (I cannot even remember quite why we were there: presumably it was a game of hide and seek—with myself hiding as far as possible from my own backgreen); when the girl I was with, without any preliminaries, crouched down and began to piddle between me and the shadowy wall, with a nonchalance which greatly impressed me even then. (We were all, to be honest, noticeably insanitary little beasts. It must have seemed so much more logical and, indeed, economical to us all, both in effort and use of space, not to waste priceless time in walking all the way back home (thereby ruining a game), climbing numberless steps and so forth, merely for a quick relief-giving burst, before travelling all the way back again. How much more admirable simply to use otherwise wholly unfrequented areas for that purpose.

All the same: there were certain rules, and it occurred to me that she was probably breaking them, and that she was therefore (for I

50

was such an appalling child) rather the less likeable for that. Yet it was, I think, although I can hardly be expected to be very certain, at this moment that I first, however fleetingly, considered that the hitherto utterly superfluous, elusive world of females, the result of a baffling and apparently pointless division of human beings into two differing groups (which no-one had so far ever bothered to enlighten me about in the slightest) might conceivably turn out to be of some interest after all. (It was only by a Sherlock Holmesian chain of inference — Conan Doyle slips obliquely into the case yet again—that I was able to work out exactly what it was that she was actually doing anyway. (I have no idea where she is now, or has been for the last 20-odd years. (And it is curious that, remembering this, and at the same time rereading in my notes that the young schoolteacher, Agnes Brown, who lived in Grant Street (she was not called at the trial (she saw two men running away)) had sometimes, from her back window, seen Miss Gilchrist, at her own back window two gardens away, and struggling to bear in mind all the while the different personal ages and public epochs involved, I feel for a moment that I am almost at the verge of understanding something very important, something unbelievably significant, about what what it is to be a woman. So, this obvious delusion hovers in the air for a moment, then passes, like everything else.)

Fifteen

I am in some danger of losing sight entirely of Oscar Slater himself, but this is because, though perhaps to say so is to be a little too flamboyant, he had nothing to do with the case. He is just the passer-by that the wall fell down on top of. Reading the accounts of the trial, one is mystified that, on any number of a number of occasions, as prosecution witness after prosecution witness delivered yet another manifest implausibility, the presiding judge did not stand up suddenly, say, "Enough is enough", and call the whole thing off. I suppose one is influenced by the knowledge of so much richly implicatory material which never came to light during the trial process—it seems to me undeniable that, on the available facts, properly presented, Slater had no case to answer—but, even so, we have the word of several observers that the "Guilty" verdict was something of a shock to the court. We also have Trench's observation (in July 1912) to the effect that the Detective Department in Glasgow were very surprised at the verdict, and practically every one of them was convinced that Slater was innocent. (Note the word "innocent". One advantage of the availability of the Not Proven verdict is of course that "Not Guilty" means "Innocent".)

"Practically everyone" is an intriguing phrase in this context. Clearly, there are exceptions, although few. And clearly these exceptions are well-placed. At least, they have the power to have their unshared suspicions acted on. It is at this point that Superintendent Ord (head of the Central Division of the Glasgow Police) falls out of the cupboard, with a knife in his back. We have it on all sides that Ord believed in Slater's guilt. Now it is, I think, no longer controversial to suggest that Ord was a man personally responsible for numerous gross breaches of procedural etiquette throughout the handling of the case, almost all of them working to Slater's direct detriment. In short, not to mince words, he did all he could to see that the blame was pinned on Slater. (His behaviour in the witness box is a particularly smooth example of misrepresentation by omission.)

It has been hinted that this interesting behavioural trait of the good Superintendent clearly suggests that he was desperately trying to shelter the (known) guilty party, (the view that both were Freemasons is, in fact, one of the more restrained interpretations here), by fixing the guilt onto someone who could easily be perceived (a

52

German Jew living off his wits in a foreign country) as being one of society's dispensables. I will not object seriously to this reading, for I think in a sense it serves him right, but I will say that the mere fact that a man pulls out all the stops to shore up, not to say fabricate, the case against another hardly suggests, of necessity, that he does not think that this other man really did it. My own view is that Ord very early on somehow got it into his head that Slater must be the murderer, and he then saw those points which in a trial might suggest his innocence, as being possible escape routes for an undoubtedly guilty man, by which means he might manage to evade his just deserts; and which it was therefore his duty (in the eyes of God, as it were, rather than than in the myopic eyes of Legal Nicety) to cut off as far as possible. (We may note that Ord accused Trench of "ruining the case" by his performance in the witness-box at the trial. What Trench in fact did was to tell the truth, regardless of how tactless such a course might prove to be. I find it difficult not to wonder what, in real terms, Ord wanted Trench to do. Presumably, not be duped into giving Slater's side what they wanted to hear—questions of "truth" hardly coming into it. This seems, to say the least, a curious way to regard the duty of giving evidence.)

Now, this view, which presumes Ord's sincerity, may make him a better man, but it surely still leaves him as being no sort of a person to run a police force. The idea that one first finds the culprit, then, as it were, reshapes the ungrateful evidence in order to provide it with a better fit, is indeed, to use Sir H. Stephen's description of the whole case, "A disgrace to a civilised country". But, of course, it is rather easy to sit at one's bay window jotting down impeccable sentiments, so let us instead (without retracting a word of what has already been said) try to examine the point a bit further.

The question is: can an investigating officer be utterly sure that a crime has been committed by a certain person, in the absence of sufficient evidence to make conviction assured? It seems to me, alas, that the answer to this is yes. (Even if only because conviction is never assured, so long as a jury has its independence.) Is he therefore invariably to be condemned for, as it were, helping the evidence along? Well, there are no doubt degrees of guilt in everything. Are we to deny that many real criminals have been convicted on the weight of adulterated evidence? (The obvious next question is: how many innocent people have been convicted ditto. (Presumably innocent people are also at times convicted on evidence which, as far as it goes, is utterly impeccable.))

I am somewhat at a disadvantage here, as it seems to me so clear that one should invariably be condemned for helping evidence along, whatever the if's and but's of any particular case. So, let me try another tack. Can we imagine a realistic scenario whereby, by the illegal invention of support for evidence otherwise insufficient, or thought to be likely to prove insufficient, to procure a conviction of an appalling criminal who, say, has (doubtless through bravado) privately admitted his guilt in a shocking crime, a situation can be reached where more good than harm is done to society? I suspect we can. We can imagine almost anything. But these things are surely objectively unquantifiable, and, as far as I understand it, the raison d'être of the legal system is to put the solution of moral problems on as objective a footing as possible, precisely to make them independent of any one person's fallible whims or intuitions—which, even though they may actually happen to operate in a benificent manner, may also at any time change, being utterly at that person's disposal, leaving the accused with no means of redress. (So that it is the being found guilty itself which makes one legally a criminal and not the committing of the crime.)

Let us consider the (ridiculous) theory that, in fact, Slater had really done it, but that the evidence was no better than it was. (It could hardly have been worse.) It is actually, on this view, difficult to know how Slater could objectively be known to be guilty. Which is to say, legally he would have to be regarded as Not Guilty, to safeguard the system in the name of those advantages which it had over a system of arbitrary justice. Yet let us suppose that Slater had in fact done it, and yet, somehow (sheer luck, presumably), the evidence was no better than it was. Would Ord have been justified, or at least less unjustified, in bending the evidence to get it to fit? As far as I can see, the answer is still an obvious "No", precisely because it must be on the evidence that his guilt or otherwise must be legally established. In the real world, we simply cannot make people guilty for the sake of argument, and solve the problem by observing that they are guilty by definition. And if the evidence was no better than it was, there would have been no reason of any sort for believing Slater to be guilty. Or, to put it another way, one has no business believing in someone's guilt independently of evidence which could be legally admissable (assuming a fair legal system and a fair trial. (But what legal system is perfectly fair? It is an interesting question to what extent technical laws of evidence may render inadmissible what would otherwise be utterly decisive considerations, and to what extent someone who objected to the nature of these technicalities could legitimately persist in beliefs which flew in the face of the technically acceptable evidence. Cases, Smith's for instance, can turn on very vexatious and debatable technical points. However, I think I have done enough to prove that I know nothing about the subject so perhaps it is time to move on.)), or, rather, for expecting someone else to be convinced by one's own belief by itself. Or, to put it another way: who am I anyway? Certainly not God. (Yes, there are people who think they are the mouthpieces of God, but enough is enough.)

My original point, as far as I can remember it, also had a more purely functional aspect. Any man who could, under the circumstances then obtaining, genuinely believe in Slater's guilt, was surely too stupid to be in a position of such power. Truly, that man must have had a remarkable potential for causing damage, and the Slater case just happens to be the one we know about. Are we to seriously believe that Oscar Slater is the only man ever to have been unjustly imprisoned because of the machinations of a man like Ord? Perhaps this was an isolated aberration of his? Truly, one can hardly fight crime adequately with a set-square and a pair of compasses, but whenever one is disposed to deal leniently with the direction of this particular affair, it is as well to remember that Trench, holder of the King's Medal, and relieved owner of a letter from the Secretary of State for Scotland which could reasonably be read as a statement of immunity from retribution, was not only unceremoniously thrown out of the police force for passing confidential documents to a lawyer (those officers tarnished by the documents of course survived untouched), but he also had a trumped-up charge of resetting thrown at him courtesy of his ex-colleagues, of so ludicrous a nature (but of a vindictiveness that can hardly be forgiven), that the judge dismissed it at sight. This episode, a characteristic amalgam of viciousness and stupidity, is rich in its implications for the Slater case. (I have read the opinion expressed, that this ploy was in fact a shrewd piece of tactics, designed to scare off Trench and Cook (the lawyer in question, also indicted), rather than undertaken with any live hope of legal success. Frankly, I doubt it, but the viciousness remains in any case. And it is hard to imagine Ord, say, breaking down in tears, gasping "No! No! We never meant anything like this to happen!", if the Court had returned a guilty verdict. It would not have been the first time an innocent man had been convicted. But no doubt Ord was not looking on the Slater case as setting some sort of precedent here.)

Sixteen

As I walked past the building in the early evening (this evening) some strip-lights were on in both of the two left-most windows of that house, and also in the windows immediately below. The sound of whirring machinery of some sort was clearly audible. Truly, we know nothing much. Who knows what might not have happened there 200 years ago, 300 years ago, before the area was built upon? Entire tribes could have been done to death there in previous light showers, for all we ever find out about it.

Which leads us naturally enough into a consideration of the reprieve—which is to say, the commutation of sentence from the original one of death by hanging. This was a curious decision, because on the supposition that Slater was guilty, there were no extenuating circumstances arguing in favour of a reprieve. The jury found Slater guilty of the cold-blooded murder of an old lady, to gain possession of her valuable jewelry. There are no obvious mitigating factors. There are no unobvious ones either. The police (who in the police, exactly?) proclaimed themelves "utterly dismayed" by the modification of sentence. Newspapers were baffled, and would continue to be so off and on for the better part of two decades. ("The public may still be excused for wondering why the royal clemency was exercised", wrote the Glasgow Herald in June 1914.)

All this puzzlement is utterly understandable, for, allowing for the moment that Slater did it, he deserved to hang as much as anyone ever did. (The counsel for the defence was quite explicit, in his final address to the jury ("certain doom", etc.), that if they found his client guilty, then the facts of the case clearly ruled out any possibility of a reprieve.) In short, the only possible mitigating factor that suggested itself to the more charitable onlookers was that of the possibility that the verdict was not a trustworthy one. However, as Slater's solicitor, Ewing Speirs, put it in the introduction to a memorial written to the Secretary of State for Scotland on his client's behalf: "If there is a doubt about his guilt, he ought to be free". In other words, what we have here is the suggestion that to declare, in effect, "Well, maybe he didn't do it after all, so we'd better just keep him in prison to be on the safe side," is not a legitimate way to field doubts about the outcome of a trial. (Of course, no-one has ever made public the official grounds for the reprieve. Well, of course not. Here we have the first glorious flowering of the official attitude to the Slater case: silence. Just be quiet and it will all go away. If you don't give them the ball, then they can't play their game. (When Trench, after his dismissal, wrote to the Secretary of State for Scotland to point out that the invitation to communicate to him what further information he knew about the case seemed to him to indicate the provision of "ample protection against any breach of discipline", he received the same eloquent response. Utter silence.))

Of course, if the powers-that-be feel unease at the justice of the outcome of a particular case, then the proper thing to do would seem to be to review the proceedings, rather than knock the sentence down a bit because of the substandard quality of the merchandise. There was, however, at the time, no such Appeal Procedure available in Scotland, such a resource presumably having to wait until the legislature in London could find the time to get round to it, since Scotland was, and indeed is, one of those (I imagine) comparatively few areas of the earth which possess an indigenous legal system, but have no indigenous capacity to create new laws, or abrogate or alter old ones. The wisdom and rightness of this hardly need to be commented on.

Of the 18 or 19 years which he spent in prison, it would be presumptuous to comment with any great claim of understanding. But it is worth pointing out that "lifers" were normally released on license after 15 years. Had Slater been guilty, he would presumably not have behaved with the fractitiousness which was apparently responsible (no-one actually says these things either, of course—which allows conspiracy theorists to enjoy yet another of those field-days which this case so lavishly provides them with) for the absence of official sanction for his release. In other words, to be slightly dramatic, he was in effect penalized for not being guilty. Until immediately before the furore created by Park's book about the case, and the subsequent journalistic activity by E.C. Palmer, there was no sign of the official mind being other than perfectly prepared to let the man stay in Peterhead Prison until he died. This is slightly chilling, as it seems a little too much to expect of a Benign Providence, that it will provide a fervent crusading journalist for everyone wrongfully convicted of a major crime.

When the storm broke following these publications—for instance, Edgar Wallace, reviewing the Park book, remarked of Slater, "He has served 19 years for a crime of which anybody but a fool might know he is guiltless", (which, incidentally, throws a baleful light on the presumed certainty of Superintendent Ord)—it was suddenly thought best to release Slater on license after all, a gesture of mercy which, thanks to its timing, was received with considerable small-mindedness on the part of many observers. It is worth pointing out

57

that Park's book, chiefly a masterly and masterful exposition of the devastating weaknesses of the case (actually, the case consists of little but weaknesses), even though it does introduce a few documents and a "new witness" (who subsequently quietly dropped from sight, which suggests she turned out to be only another of those wierd souls who haunt the peripheries of lurid crimes—but I must try to find out more about her) is in essence merely the restatement, in suitably resonant form, of what was already public knowledge. That is to say, it does not bring light into a previously dark room: rather, it merely switches on lights which were there all the time.

And yet, after all, an Appeal Court of five judges did indeed eventually consider the case. A certain amount of new evidence was led, a certain amount was not led—Lambie refused to come over from the U.S.A. to attend—and long disquisitions were delivered for and against the submission, proposed on four counts, that the original verdict should not be allowed to stand.

This court, of course, eventually decided that the original verdict indeed could not be allowed to stand. But it did so in a manner uniquely ill-suited to provide a graceful termination to the whole affair. That is to say: the first three counts were rejected, and the decision was founded entirely on the fourth count, the one which suggested that the trial judge's final summing-up was prejudicial to the prisoner. This was accepted, and the verdict of the trial was held to be invalid, through a misdirection of the trial judge on a point of law. Now, it is not this that one objects to as such. The fairness of the decision on this point must surely be clear to everyone except perhaps the immediate family circle of the Lord Guthrie (the judge in question—to whom, by the by, the first (1910) edition of the account of the trial, by William Roughead, was dedicated, and whose full-length portrait formed the frontispiece thereto). Indeed, this is part of the problem. The inadequacy of the judge's summing-up had been remarked upon for almost twenty years, ever since he actually made the speech in question. (The version given in the first edition mentioned above was actually revised by the judge himself prior to publication. There seem to be no gross alterations, but, surely the idea is intrinsically somewhat distasteful? (One would give much for a version of the famous trials of the other criminological Oscar, rewritten by Wilde himself.))

To give only one example: the memorial written by Slater's solicitors, mentioned above, explicitly points to the final summing-up as being prejudicial to the accused. This was in 1910. Subsequently, high-placed official after high-placed official impeturbably bats back enquiries about Slater with the remark that it was felt that there was no reason to interfere with the admirable state of affairs at present obtaining. And then, quite suddenly, in 1928, it is discovered that in fact Ewing Spiers was right after all, and the judge's summing-up clearly could not be allowed to stand ("a clear misdirection in law" was the phrase used.) One might say that for the entire 18 years that Slater was in Peterhead, there was a key in the lock of his door, but no-one passing could spare the time to turn it and let him out. (I have yet to read of anyone who claimed that the "clear misdirection in law" was not just as blatant in 1909 as in 1928, and would be genuinely interested, and not a little surprised, to discover any possible argument in favour of this contention.)

It was, however, not the fault of the Court of Appeal as such that it had not been convoked earlier (although I seem to recall that two of the five judges had previously held offices in which capacity reports on the Slater case had been forwarded to them). And they did at least annul the earlier verdict, even if with less brio than one might have hoped for, or indeed, have legitimately expected, given the nature of their remit. (As far as I can see, there is nowhere any such thing as an unequivocal official statement of the extremely obvious, if inconvenient, truth, that Slater just did not do it and never had done it. I agree that it is not easy to envisage the circumstances under which such a statement could come into being, but for some reason I still feel its absence.)

Yet, the judgement of the Appeal Court is in one more way extremely striking. Obviously, Slater must have got the money he lived on from somewhere, and, as I understand it, his own version of this is that he lived on what he won as a gambler. This sounds unlikely, but it is far from impossible, and I do not see how one could be certain that it is untrue. The man in the street view (a different man from the Watcher, presumably) is that he was also a pimp. Now, this is probably not the most improbable speculation that one will ever hear in the whole course of one's life, but it is one thing to be aware of the possibility, and quite another to assume it to be proved. (Slater himself always denied it in uncompromising terms, which is not surprising of course, but not utterly negligible either.) The evidence for this mode of Slater's supplementing his income comes in the cross-examination of the *defence* witness, Cameron, one of the few of Slater's cronies who was a local. On being pressed as to knowledge of Slater's source of wealth, he volunteered the information that he had heard that Oscar, like many others who came to Glasgow, lived off etc. etc. etc., as above. Truly, he could with as much legal force have said that he had heard that Oscar was a neurosurgeon. The remarks are, of course, mere hearsay, treating of events outwith the witness's first-hand knowledge, and thus, however suggestive or controversial, they are legally worthless.

59

(Reading the man's evidence, it is rather a shock to see how unobtrusively these three or four lines slip by. They are possibly the most damaging moment of the entire trial, but past they go, unmarked, in normal type and spacing, like an exchange about the weather.)

Now, the submissions of the defence show that it obviously had great hopes that it would be on this very point, and the illegitimate use made of it by both the Lord Advocate and the presiding judge in his summing-up, that the trial would be declared invalid, as observations had been so copiously founded on what was inadmissible evidence. In fact, something like the reverse happened. Not only did the Appeal Judges imperturbably accept that this immorality of Slater's private life had been proved by the evidence—a strange notion—but, freely dropping remarks like "the appellant's disreputable relations with the female members of his household", it, as it were, elevated the totally innocent hired maidservant Catherine Schmalz to, in effect, the rank of prostitute too, under Slater's tutelage—something which even the prosecution had failed to think of at the trial. There is not so much as a whisper in the evidence led (or evidence not led, for that matter) to suggest that this could possibly be the case. And this occurs, not in the copy of some hard-pressed and imaginative journalist, but in the considered statement of five of the judiciary system's leading lights. Scottish justice: the envy of the world!

Seventeen

It is interesting to walk along these streets in the evenings, on the way to the library, intending to write more about events of nearly a century ago. As I did so this evening, I recalled Slater's remark when, months after the events, he was trying to recollect what he had been doing at the time of the murder: "To me that night is just like any other night". So it seemed as it passed. One then thinks: well, tonight is just like any other night too. And what if another such murder had just taken place. It is only at this point that one begins even to look at the various passers-by with any intensity.

Truly, it is hard to believe that a jury should be asked to concern itself with such nonsense as the testimony of Mary Barrowman. A man raced past her on a dark night, colliding with her (according to her later version), and she was certain Slater was that man. Indeed, impelled by an urge difficult to account for, she turned and followed him a little way down the road. She then turned again, and went back down the road in her original direction.

It is obvious to me, (as it has been to others before me), that Barrowman was never even there at the time of the murder. To begin with, nobody saw her, and that street was full of people looking desperately in one direction after another before she, on her own evidence, would have had time to leave it. The likeliest view is that, to quote her original police statement, with a little judicious editing, "After leaving (an address where she had delivered a package containing boots, to get to which she had gone down West Princes Street). . . I (again) passed. . . 49 West Princes Street, (where I first heard of the) murder, and I then thought of. . .". In short, the girl delayed her return home excessively by lingering too long at the scene of an exciting crime, and, when she eventually got home, she sought to deflect parental ire by inventing a completely fictitious story, with not a thought in her mind for anything but surviving the immediate domestic crisis. Tomorrow would take care of itself.

The evidence of her mother, who preceded her as a witness at the trial, is interesting. "I took no notice, because I thought it was just a story, and I said, 'Now, Mary, hold your tongue, because you do not know anything about it'. (Sage advice indeed, and true. Would that it had been taken.) There was no more said that night." (A murderer bumped against the girl, but she said no more about it. There ought to be a song of that name.) And here we come to another

61

of those awful coincidences which, with the brooch, the domicile so near by, the timing of his departure, seem to suggest that the Laws of Probability had taken a personal dislike to Slater. (Perhaps it objected to his style of gaming.) It just so happened that a detective in the Northern Department of the Glasgow Police lived in the flat immediately above the Barrowmans. Two days later, meeting him on the stair (another meeting on a stairway), the mother mentioned to him what her daughter claimed to have seen, and Detective McGimpsey set the official machinery in motion.

(Presumably the mother no longer thought the daughter was just telling stories? God knows. Perhaps she thought no harm could come of it, and it might just do some good. How can we tell? (There is a story that Mary Barrowman later claimed that her mother was an alcoholic, who put her up to it for the reward money, but, frankly, I would want a second opinion to Mary Barrowman's on this. (Have we not all, in childhood, told a lie which suddenly developed an entire ecosystem of complications, which we had to invent some sort of plausible way through? I suspect this is the case here. I would have no doubt that Barrowman was a considerable liar. (Most notably, she shared a cabin with Lambie on the 12-day trip over to the United States, to identify Slater. When asked at the trial, had they discussed the case on the way over, she answered, No. (It was never mentioned. Not once in twelve days. Not a word of it.))))) *(Similarly Detective Inspector Pyper, crossing in the same cabin as the witness Adams, does not revert to the subject "in any way" [trial].)*

However, Barrowman was a 15 year-old girl, and she could be forgiven for not understanding the implications of what she was doing. As Lambie was 23, her behaviour is slightly less susceptible to indulgence. She too, it seems to me, lied fairly freely, but it also seems to me that she too was to some extent caught up against her will in a process fuelled by the irrational certainty of part of the police force, and, perhaps, the Procurator Fiscal (i.e., the supposedly objective arbiter who decides, independently of vested interests, which criminal proceedings shall be brought to trial, and which, for whatever reason, should be dropped). It seems that these men overrode the obvious suggestions being put out by both females, that they would welcome the opportunity to back out as graciously as possible, and instead saw to it that their facts were consistent, that they knew in advance what Slater would look like, and all the 1001 little details that go into the everyday administration of justice. (Perhaps this explains the reports of Agnes Brown claiming that attempts had been made to get her to alter her story—otherwise so inconvenient for the prosecution—to come into line with Barrowman's fable. (Note also the remark of Mrs. Liddell (Adams's sister, and one of the "Watcher" witnesses), a propos the fabric of this elsuive gentleman's coat: "It was a thick coat. I have stuck to that all along, and I will stick to it still"—which, as Roughead points out, rather suggests that someone had been (perhaps persistently) attempting to improve her memory.)

Lambie is truly a law unto herself. But she will have to wait for a moment, for I stopped writing for the day at that point, and spent much of the next day looking through bound volumes of old newspapers. Which is to say, the Glasgow Evening Times for December 1908, and the Evening News for the whole period from the murder on the 21st of December, to the reprieve at the end of May 1909. (The first 1909 volume of the Evening Times was not available, being in too bad a condition for issue to the public. This was the greater pity in that it was the more interesting journal of the two. (Or, for that matter—since it is still published—far more interesting than it is in its present incarnation. (By the way, after assiduously turning through the large volume of the Evening News for 1909, my labours were crowned with the discovery that the page at which the account of the trial culminated had been torn out. A word of thanks to the anonymous vandal.)

There was much of interest to read and reflect on, and a few suggestions were made at the time which seem never to have been picked up; but I shall go at once to what it taught me about Barrowman. Objectively, nothing whatever emerged to make me doubt the version which I have given above, but the Glasgow News did run the occasional photograph (including a striking vignette of Slater on January the 13th (this was months before the trial)), and I thus now know what Barrowman looked like. Not to labour the point, she was a strikingly good-looking girl. (Indeed, neither Barrowman, Annie Armour (the ticket girl at Kelvinbridge), nor Lambie herself, was a woman from whom one would rapidly avert one's gaze for aesthetic reasons, and we may as well point out that the jury consisted of 15 males, most of them under 40.) In particular, there is a charming photograph of her arriving at the Edinburgh High Court which is a completely unposed shot. She is some way in front of a pair of rigid elders who, I presume, are her parents. (Which to say, her adoptive parents. She was adopted at nine days of age. By the way, typical of the thought-provoking information content of this whole case is the fact that her hours of work as a delivery girl were from 9 a.m. till 8 p.m.)

She appears to be laughing at something. At the time of the final agitation for Slater's release, she is described as being "now a stout, middle-aged matron", "living in the backwoods of Glasgow", but here we suddenly see a bright lively girl, dressed, doubtless, at the height of fashion, and obviously the most modern thing in the modern world. It can at times be difficult to take the realness of the past seriously, particularly the recent past—for one thing, their newspapers had such funny lay-outs—but I may say that, looking at that photograph, the awareness that I was gazing at another today, another this moment, hit me with a force that had me somewhat disorientated. Certainly, I was no longer looking at my own happy little liar. Or rather, I suddenly hoped I wasn't. (Truly, the advantages of being there in court on the spot while it happens must cut both ways. Is a juryman not to notice a new hat? How big a gap lies betweeen the theory of a trial and the practice? (In particular, the assumption that, once a damaging but inadmissible fact has been uttered, and the judge directs the jury to dismiss it from their minds, to behave as if it had never been revealed, the jury is actually then able to do so. Common sense suggests that it must at least be extraordinarily difficult, and one could, I think, hardly begin to estimate the number of times when an illegitimate submission has been deliberately made, in the full knowledge that it will be ruled impermissible, but trusting that it will produce an afterglow all the same. (Ord understands this particularly well, as his behaviour at the trial all too clearly shows. "I have other information"—that is, to suggest that Slater was travelling with London rather than Liverpool tickets (to help throw pursuers off the scent)—"but that is not evidence," he says helpfully, thereby making the (quite illegitimate) point anyway.)

I thus began to run over in my mind some aspects of her role that I had not fully appreciated before. Barrowman's greatest contribution was the "twisted nose". This is (in more ways than one) an arresting phrase. Notice, she did not say broken nose, or bashed nose, or hooked nose, or any other phrase more accurately descriptive of Slater's, alas, somewhat distinctive proboscis. (It was pure bad luck for Slater, of course, that he was a German Jew with a broken nose. Barrowman had never seen him until the extradition proceedings in New York began. (I remember, in this connection, reading—in Hunt's book I think—that prisoners who emerged from Peterhead Prison reported that all this "twisted nose" business had led them seriously astray in their attempts to put a face to their famous new arrival, Slater.)) No, it was, in the words of the police, "lightly turned to one side. The witness thinks the twist is to the right side". (Incidentally, did it never occur to the police to wonder why their preternaturally gifted eye-witness, able otherwise to describe in the minutest detail the garb and appearance of a man hurrying past her at night, could not remember for certain this detail of the most obvious feature of his face? She saw that his nose was twisted, but could not remember for certain in which direction? Perhaps it was twisted in both directions at once?)

Now, this detail, like many others, largely vanished from sight during the trial, but it was the subject of an interesting interchange at the extradition proceedings in New York, when Barrowman, in response, gave out the information that never before in all her life had she seen a man in Glasgow with a twisted nose. The next question was: How old are you? I noted down these circumstances from Park's book, but did not quite see the force of them then. (It might be said here, that, as far as Slater is concerned, the American system of justice comes out spectacularly ahead of the Scottish one.)

I take it now that the inference is that this hitherto unseen facial peculiarity is an invention on the girl's part, and a particularly flagrant one; and it was describing something, in her experience, utterly bizarre, and hardly reconcilable with Slater's own striking but not so utterly unprecedented appearance. But I do not think that this ball quite stops rolling here. In my view, Barrowman had not the least notion that the line which she spun to her mother would end up with her being confronted by a battery of detectives. (Of course, she could have admitted the lie there and then (perhaps she did, says the distant but advancing voice of insanity) but I do not for a moment concede that the fact that she did not do so makes it likelier that she was telling the truth.) Finding that this was the case, the best plan, while preserving dignity and at the same time escaping the danger of identifying any suspect the police might bring before her, would be to invent a non-existent person. This is no doubt all over-heated nonsense, (who knows what was going through her mind at any particular moment—it is just as likely that the detail was an attempt to give individual life to an otherwise rather abstract characterization), but I suspect that, by giving an utterly normal male an impossible feature like a twisted nose, Barrowman was attempting to back gracefully out of the limelight. (There is, incidentally, a closely argued letter printed in one of the newspapers soon afterwards which explains the whole thing, with appalling plausibility, as being the result of the assailant's wearing a false nose (freely available at theatrical shops), which had become twisted on the hectic journey downstairs! This piece of lunacy is so brilliant, and so carefully thought out, that fear forbids me from thinking about it for too long.)

Finally, I wonder to what extent Barrowman's attested cocksureness and tendency to impertinence was not in fact encouraged by the knowledge that the forces of law and order were wholly committed in all their majesty to upholding the truth of (or had been taken in by) her own absurd version of events.

Eighteen

I suppose I ought to turn my attention to Lambie now. The belief that, if one waits merely for another day or so, that should be enough for a complete understanding of the case, is a seductive one, but, in the end, pretty ludicrous self-flattery. I believe that the old lady was indeed alone in the house when Lambie left for the paper. That is by no means certain, but, in a case already so full of complexities, there is no point in adding to them without good reason. Besides, I suspect that Lambie's departure was in itself something in the nature of a signal. (Though this may be even less likely.) It seems to me, however, that to dismiss all the talk there is of a young man watching the house from the street as being mere retrospective invention— although quite possibly correct—is nonetheless an unnecessarily drastic step to take. It is perhaps too cavalier to assume that these are all bona fide sightings, all of the same person, and always of someone waiting for Helen Lambie to leave the house, at a set time, so that this person might approach it, but there does on occasion seem to have been a young man hanging about that corner waiting for something to happen, and so perhaps we can claim him just once for our purposes.

More than that: freely piling unfettered speculation upon unfettered speculation, I must say I have always been slightly confused by the somewhat tautologous arrangement in effect that night with regard to Lambie's message-going. She went out, bought a newspaper, returned, and was all set (apparently this was not an unusual arrangement, but I have not been able to find out whether it was actually normal, or even invariable) to hand in the newspaper at once to her mistress, then pick up a half-sovereign which had been given her, or put on the table, for the purpose, and go back out and get the remainder of her shopping. Presumably she would thereafter immediately retrace her steps to St. George's Road.

This seems to me to be a flamboyantly baroque method of buying in the necessaries. There is no very obvious reason for not completing the task in a single journey. Of course, the world is not a logical theorem, but if one wished or was duty bound to talk to someone occasionally, in conditions of strict secrecy, and with whom one did not wish to be left alone for more than a few minutes, for whatever reason, then this would seem to be the best time for which to arrange it.

We will see in the sequel exactly who this man might be, and what these discussions will have been. For the meanwhile, let us return to Lambie. She herself returns to the stairway, finding the main-door ajar, and a couple of wet footprints on the stair. Even so, she is surprised to see Mr. Adams there. (In 27 or so years, he has been up that stairway seven or eight times(!), according to his evidence.) Mr Adams expresses fears about her mistress's safety, in the light of certain loud noises, perhaps warning knocks, which he has heard. Now, Miss Gilchrist was known to be in great dread of intruders. More than that: a week or so before this, Helen Lambie had, without invitation, gone to visit her previous employer, a woman who lived a good distance away (well out of Glasgow), and whom she by then had not seen for over three years. (This woman was not at the trial, her statement becoming available to the defence only on the fourth day of proceedings.) To this woman she had imparted the quite startling information that something strange was going on, that jewels were being hidden in odd places, and that Miss Gilchrist had told her she feared she was going to be murdered.

Might it not be imagined, given all these circumstances, that Helen Lambie would give a hint of nervousness? I think it might, but apparently she didn't. A propos the noise, she observed that it was probably the pulleys, suspecting that they might have fallen down in the kitchen (which they seem to have done not long before). Plainly, the truth of what had happened did not cross her mind, nor even the possibility of that truth. (I think I am safe in assuming that, if it had, her demeanour would have shown it.)

Very good. She unlocks the door with two keys. (Presumably this is an automatic necessity from the outside whenever the door is closed.) She enters the house, with Adams remaining politely on the landing outside. Where does she go first? Is it not to be expected that she will at once go into the room where she left her old, possibly threatened mistress? Apart from anything else, it is the first door she comes to. (All the same—this may simply show how very far any thought of threat was from her mind. (Which casts an ambiguous light on that talk during her visit to the former mistress of hers, assuming it existed.)) But no: she carries on, past the door, past the clock, and, just as she is about to step into the tiny sub-hall leading to the kitchen door etcetera, a man emerges from the corresponding recess on the other side, walks affably towards Adams at the door, keeping unnaturally close to the wall as he does so, then passes the naturally disconcerted Adams, and races down the stairway.

This incident has, for want of a better word, a Shakespearian quality to it. I can still remember the shudder that passed through me when I reached this moment on first reading a detailed account of the case. The presumed murderer walks away, smiling towards the chief witnesses, and is never caught. Truly, this must be some sort of first for the Glasgow Police. Or so one hopes.

Well, let us do what everyone else did, and let him go. What choice have we now? That Adams did nothing is wholly understandable, as he was utterly unfamiliar with the house and its visitors (it works out on average at something like one visit every four years), and he would therefore take his cue from Lambie. The man, he later said, looked and behaved like a young male relative of the house. (That is, most probably, exactly what he was.) As Lambie did and said nothing, he felt himself not called upon to interfere. He first suspected something was wrong only when the man began to bolt down the stairs.

Let us leap ahead at this point, not unlike the murderer himself, to a moment in 1914, during the Enquiry set up to investigate the evidence tended by John Thomson Trench, the main point of which was that, in effect, in ten minutes time, ten minutes after the man left, Helen Lambie would be arriving, almost hysterical, at the nearby house of a niece of Miss Gilchrist, where she would identify by name who it was that she had just seen. (At this enquiry, everyone, with monotonous regularity and uniformity of speech, denied that such a naming had taken place; although they all agreed that the visit itself had occurred—a visit which went for nothing during the trial itself. (As far as I remember, it was not once mentioned. None of the, by now 7 or 8, newspaper accounts of the fatal night which I have seen mention it either.)) In this farcical and disgraceful affair, during which one would say that 90% of the witnesses perjured themselves, except for the bizarre fact that it was not conducted under oath, Lambie, recounting her preferred version of the night's events, said, "I did not know the man and never saw him before". At this point, something almost incredible occurred: to wit, Mr. Gardner Millar, K.C., Sheriff of Lanarkshire, who was, at least theoretically, conducting the enquiry, interrupted her to ask a question. (Perhaps he simply forgot where he was.) He enquired, "Why did you not ask him what he was doing there?" And her answer? "I never suspected anything wrong." She was then allowed to continue with her polished narration, unimpeded any further.

It is reasonable to suppose that, if the circumstances were indeed such as she later claimed them to be—and yet, even so, she still suspected nothing was amiss, then she showed a lack of imagination so monumental that it almost deserves to become proverbial. Indeed, that she finally managed to perceive that something was wrong on seeing the old lady's battered body is more than we had a right to expect from her, if this performance is to be our guide. (At the trial, if my notes are accurate, she had also been asked, why did you not ask him what he was doing there (it is in many ways the absolutely central question in the case), and she had replied, I never suspected there was anything wrong. So, at least she was being consistent. Or, to put it another way, she hadn't been able to think up a better answer in four years.)

Really, unless she neither heard nor saw the man leave, her strange reticence of behaviour requires explanation. Adams at the trial stated, during re-examination (so it's just as well he was re-examined, isn't it?), "Yes, she saw the man, because she stood and stared and did not open her mouth". Further asked, "Was she plainly taken aback?", he replied, "Yes, thoroughly. That was my impression." I see no reason at all to doubt the veracity of any of this. So, she was considerably surprised, but she *still* said and did nothing. Let us suppose the ridiculous for one moment: let us suppose that, say, Oscar Slater had walked out under such circumstances. Can we at all reasonably expect that Lambie would have reacted thus? (This is, in effect, what the prosecution alleged.) What—not so much as a "Who are you?" Not the least gasp or scream, at the sight of this (very) strange man whom she had never seen before? And would she then, after he had left, running away down the stairway, have continued to say nothing at all, and have gone, not into the drawing-room, where she had left her vulnerable old mistress, but into the kitchen instead, to inspect the pulleys? Well, I suppose honesty compels us to admit that this is possible. It conforms to the laws of physics, at least. More than that it is difficult to claim for it with any confidence.

I think we may safely say that she was taken aback by something—but not by who the man was. In fact, the circumstances are unusual enough even if the departer is someone one knows. To observe someone walk out of the house past one, from an unexpected area, and without so much as saying a word, must be a little disconcerting, no matter who the person might be. One would not necessarily react at once, even if one were unaccompanied, waiting instead to see quite what the surprising apparition had in mind. It is worth recalling here part of the statement which Lambie, now Gillon, tracked down to Peoria, Illinois, made (according to the newspaper that printed it during the furore of the pre-release period) in 1927. "I had my reasons for not looking too closely. The man I thought I saw coming out of the flat had been visiting Miss Gilchrist on another occasion, and I happened to mention his name to my mistress afterwards. She flew into a temper with me, and told me that if I ever displayed the slightest curiosity again about any of her visitors, she would dismiss me without a character." (Note the "happened to mention". It looks as if she was being just a little too nosey, and was not subtle enough to get round the old lady.)

Under these circumstances, it might be the most politic course of action open to her to do absolutely nothing, but concentrate her efforts instead in gently shaking off Mr. Adams without letting him know anything he shouldn't. After all, he is very much an outsider himself. Thus, she continues on her way into the kitchen, finds for no doubt the last time, that all there is as it should be, and calls out as much to her diffident comrade, hoping he will take the hint and depart. Adams, however, is more alarmed than she supposes, and he shows no inclination to leave without further reassurance. So she looks into the bedroom, where the fire is lit, without even sufficient attention to notice the scattered documents, and comes back out. At this point, the interfering old busybody impetuously calls out: "What about your mistress?" Well, there is nothing for it now. She must go into the room where her mistress is, and perhaps put up with a certain unpleasantness. (I have become uncomfortably aware even as I write how closely this behaviour mimics the desire to stay away from the venue of an unsavoury sight, but I can't think this is a serious possibility.)

Instead, what she sees is something unimaginable. Her mistress is not, as usual, sitting in the chair, reading. There will be no sharp remarks about her having caught sight of the visitor. The fire crackles and burns, much as it did fifteen minutes ago. But by now there is much spattered material around it and above it. A rug has been placed upon the old lady's face. This head, covered by the rug, is nearest to her feet, for the old lady has fallen backwards from the surroundings of the fire. According to the evidence of the trial in the following year, what she shouts out is, "Oh; come here!"

(This last phrase, also part of Adams's evidence, has truth written all over it. (I have always been fascinated by this rug over the face. Was it an instinctive reaction on the killer's part to cover the worst evidence of his crime? I don't know. Was it motivated by the desire to spare Lambie the sight of her gruesomely treated mistress? Most unlikely. Was it intended to draw whoever next arrived on the scene—that is to say, almost certainly Lambie—into the room to find out more of what had happened by introducing an element of obscurity, thereby enabling the killer to walk out past the open door?

After all, if the killer knew the house, he presumably expected Lambie to arrive alone. And, having done so, she would surely make directly for the living-room, (the living-room!), and he would be able to get out unseen. I expect that that was what he was waiting for. It is all so haphazard. Did he hear the two of them speaking outside? What if Lambie had gone into the living-room first, and cried out? Was the man improvising? If so, he did it brilliantly, but the situation favoured him more than he had a right to expect. (There is the suggestion in an early newspaper report that the murderer might have been defeated by the contrary motion of the two locks on the door, and had to wait for whoever came in next to let him out. This is a scarifyingly magnificent image, but a little forced all the same. Besides which, the killer did not break cover quickly enough to prevent Lambie from closing the door behind her again, if she had wanted to.) At any rate, at just about the moment when he judged Helen Lambie would be entering the vital room (perhaps she appeared in sight just after he elected to move) he decided to walk out, pinning his trust in a general confusion. I must say I get the impression that whoever thus quietly broke cover, callous murderer though he certainly was, was also, alas, a distinctly intelligent man.

Nineteen

I have discovered a puzzling line among my notes: "She (Lambie) had been up at some friends of Miss Gilchrist", which I suspect might come from the testimony of Police Constable Walker at the trial. If so, it is the only such mention, and the Defence did not pick it up (as, in fairness, they could hardly be expected to, not knowing a word of the A.B. business.) It was, I think, this constable who made the first accredited (?) sighting of Slater the Watcher, in West Princes Street, on December the 1st. This custodian on the beat claimed to have seen Slater several times in the neighbourhood, and we need hardly doubt this, as Slater was a striking, obviously foreign type (a George Grosz drawing *avant la lettre* in some respects) and it was part of the P.C.'s job to notice such things. But, of course, this utterly unmistakable foreignness of Slater's dress and general appearance (not quite as striking, perhaps, as that of the party of six Eskimoes who, I learn from the newspapers, were in Glasgow at that time, but instantly evident nonetheless in the ambience of greater sartorial distinctiveness then prevailing) was remarked on by no-one else. Consider this simple point. Neither, Lambie, Barrowman, Adams, or, indeed, any of the "Watcher"-watchers at any time suggested that the object of their scrutiny was distinctly, or even somewhat, foreign. When Slater's Jewish nose was thought assimilable to Barrowman's "twisted" fantasy, then that was permissible, but the rest of Slater's distinctively alien physiognomy and appearance counted for nothing. Yet surely Park's point, that this single fact would have entitled a jury to have voted the rejection of the evidence as to identity *in toto*, is undeniable. Are we to listen seriously to the identificatory evidence of people who do not notice the most strikingly obvious quality of the identifyee? (Adams, of course, never said that Slater was the man; only that they were very like each other. He was not wearing his spectacles. (Even so, the Lord Advocate, nothing daunted, in his closing address to the jury specifically stated: "And he says that the prisoner was the man"—(I find myself unaccountably swinging round towards the belief that the Eskimoes did it)—rather on the grounds, as far as I understand him (not far, I grant you) that the witness is a diffident man, who, if he hadn't been so fastidious, would have made a quite positive identificiation, and so we may as well (as it were) remedy this defect in his character for him. He'll thank us for it when he is older.) One of the witnesses identified Slater from a view of his back, 13 yards away. One identified Slater as the (clean-shaven) Watcher from a photograph showing him wearing a moustache—no room for doubt there. One had not been positive at the time, but had been thinking it over, and had come to the conclusion (I am not making this up) that it really had been him after all.

But this Police Constable, to get back to him, is instructive on this point. You see, on his first identification of Slater, as a man walking slowly through West Princes Street, the Constable testified that he had mistaken him for someone else—to wit, one Isaac Paradise (who was actually a witness at the trial—Slater ordered house furniture from him in the shop he worked in, which happened to be Stuart and Stuart's—directly underneath Slater's residence). Now, this Isaac Paradise (a name which is almost too good to be true) also happened to be a German Jew. You see the point. The policeman mistook Slater for someone else who was and who looked like a German Jew. Ergo, obviously Slater, to the Police Constable at least, also looked like a German Jew.

Well, yes; but of course this does not explain why only the P.C. noticed this. (That is to say, alone of the witnesses called at the trial. Other people, like the laundry assistant Mary Cooper (a name which sounds so like my mother's—which last is pronounced, in effect, Mary Coopner), who identified Slater on sight as a foreigner, were not called. Why confuse the issue further?) Further, it raises the interesting point that, if the P.C. signalled in a friendly manner to his well-known acquaintance across the street (which is how he describes it), then discovered it was not him after all, his ability to identify people is self-evidently far from flawless. However, this cuts both ways, so let us ask instead if it is not wonderfully neat (though scarcely surprising) that the only evidence tending to point to Slater belonging to the distinctive human group that he did in fact belong to should come from a member of the police force? How overjoyed Superintendent Ord, for instance, must have been when P.C. Walker diffidently took him aside, and whispered into his astonished ear the curious details of this misapprehension of his, which, as it happens, goes some way to patching up a gaping flaw in the case.

A propos of absolutely nothing, let us turn to a remarkable coincidence which emerges in the testimony of one of the Watcher witnesses, one of several women called MacHaffie. She was one of a family (apparently all female) who spent a lot of their time looking out the window (as no doubt they have every right to). Now, the striking thing here is that the Watcher at one point *actually came to their door*. He asked if anyone of the name of Anderson lived there. No-one of that name did, which is perhaps just as well. He

73

then turned and went back downstairs, passing (perhaps even brushing against?) another MacHaffie sister who was just coming upstairs. (Another meeting on a stairway).

Now, the point here, of course, is that Slater took up residence in 69 St. George's Road, under the name of A. Anderson, Dentist. Anderson, I repeat, is precisely the name which the man at the door enquired after. Whoever this man was, assuming him (for the rest of the sentence at least) to exist, he was not Slater. Is this coincidence of names not quite extraordinary? Anderson is certainly a not unusual name, but it is not Smith or MacDonald (and, even if it were, the accident would still be worth remarking on quietly). Truly, this is all very mysterious. But of the thousands of available surnames which this perhaps only slightly or partially real caller could have enquired after, only two, Slater or Anderson, could have materially improved the standing of the official case. Help pours in towards the police version from all sides. (I don't know why, but thinking of this persuades me, for the moment at least, that the brightest and best of the police handling the official line in this case were unscrupulous men, without even the dubious excuse of being geniuses.)

(One further point, before I leave this section, which I had originally intended would be a further exploration of Lambie's behaviour. This witness was asked if the caller had had a foreign accent, and she replied: No, he hadn't. This, apart from anything else, makes it quite clear that it was not Slater, whose foreign accent was well attested, and would soon, furthermore, be clearly displayed to the jury after they had found him guilty. It was also rather a blow to those conspiracy theorists who suppose that this incident is a fantasy inspired by the police, since, obviously, the witness could have been instructed to answer the question affirmatively. They are thus forced to shore up their theory with such additional suppositions as that the incident really happened, but the name involved was forgotten, and remembered only under official prompting; or that the official mind was too stupid, or not sufficiently alert, to anticipate this line of questioning. It is simpler to believe that the events happened as described, or that this was what the witness remembered as happening, prompted by God knows what, (for instance, in the newspapers). (I should add, in conclusion, that, to the best of my knowledge, this point about accent almost escaped everyone. It was, as far as I recall, elicited from the witness by THE JUDGE HIMSELF, just before she stood down. If so, this is a bonus mark for Lord Guthrie. But I must check this.)

74

Twenty

I'm afraid my sins are beginning to find me out. I discover, deeper in my notes, the remark, "I did not go straight back to the house; I went and told Miss Birrell, a niece of Miss Gilchrist's, what happened." This, it must be, was what Lambie said at the trial. If I look further, perhaps I'll find that A.B. was mentioned at the trial too. (No; I think this must more or less exhaust the references to this significant visit during the trial. In other words, the fact of the visit was indeed established. But, beyond the mere fact, nothing was revealed about the incident.)

A vital question, of course, is whether Lambie, during this visit to Miss Birrell, said what Trench subsequently reported her to have said. I doubt if we should read too much into the mere fact of the visit. I suppose Miss Birrell was just about the nearest relative (as the crow flies) of Miss Gilchrist (though there were other relatives only two doors further down the same street), and the inclination to run there might have been strongly present anyway. (Even though Miss Gilchrist's estrangement from her relatives (not one of whom, by the way, testified at the trial) was well-known. (Apparently her father, a well-to-do civil engineer, had left a disproportionate amount of money to Marion in his will (she had three sisters, I think), and the family more or less cut her off because of that, or because of some unknown line of events of which this was the culmination.)) One wonders when, if ever, Lambie had been there before. And one would certainly not have been surprised if she had felt that the circumstances compelled her to remain where she was. (After all, she merely stayed at Miss Birrell's for a few minutes, and then came back alone. It cannot have been sheer terror of being in *that house* which drove her off.))

I do not see how we can reasonably interpret the Trench episode without assuming that someone is lying. If so, we must try to decide who it is. Now, as on one side of the evidence we have the detective Trench, and, on the other, almost everyone else, (there must be about twenty of them whose testimony contradicts Trench's), it might seem that the choice is easily made. But let us consider Trench, and also consider what motives he might have had for lying. Here we have a man who was awarded the King's Medal, for which he was recommended by the Chief Constable of Glasgow, for exemplary and meritorious service in a career during which he rose from Constable

75

to Detective-Lieutenant. He is married, with six children to support, and is due a pension on retirement. Recently, he has distinguished himself by his work on the Broughty Ferry murder case (November, 1912—Slater has already spent at least three years in prison), which has intensified his misgivings about cases such as Slater's, which hinge on questions of identity. (Briefly: the Broughty Ferry case is almost a carbon copy of the Gilchrist murder, although it lacked two of the most intriguing aspects of the latter: a man walking out past witnesses, and the long-term imprisonment of an innocent person on the charge. An eccentric old lady, living alone, was battered to death in a well-protected house. Nothing was stolen. (The crime, by the way, was never solved. Another parallel with the Slater case.) A dozen or so people who believed themselves to be witnesses identified the culprit from photographs shown to them by the police. To the best of my recollection, identification parades strengthened them in their beliefs. (Did not one of them tearfully say: "I know I am putting a rope around the man's neck by saying this, but it was him"? I find this in my notes, and I strongly suspect that it belongs here.) A 300-page precognition was accumulated in the case. The accused man was a tramp who could not substantiate his whereabouts, except to make the self-evidently ludicrous claim that he had been in Antwerp (!) at the time and that he had pawned his waistcoat there. Trench took the precaution of going to Antwerp (apparently no-one else thought it worth putting themselves to such pointless trouble), where he scoured the local pawnshops and—found the man's waistcoat! The man was (perhaps with a certain amount of reluctance) released. (But supposing he had been found Guilty, and had hanged: would we so much as scent an injustice now? Of course we wouldn't. Not even the person who next walked around Belgium in his waistcoat. (It is worth observing that here we have Trench in point of fact "ruining" another perfectly adequately solved police case. (And notice the pawnshop. But for this institution, this man, Warner, might well have hanged, and Slater might well have lived out his life in the United States, as Lambie subsequently did.)))

It seems clear to me that the only reason why Trench would act as he did would be because he genuinely believed that what he said was true, and the continuing inactivity weighed on his conscience. Park published a photograph of an excerpt from the diary kept by Trench (a procedural necessity for a detective) which showed that he had been sent to Miss Birrell's two days after the murder. (Other documents which Trench claimed likewise testified to this visit had since vanished. How curious.) Furthermore, another detective, by name another Cameron, during the 1914 "A.B." Enquiry, corroborated that Trench had told him at the time that Miss Birrell had said to him that Lambie had said to her on the night of the murder that the man who passed her in the lobby was like A.B. This is comically hearsay to read, but it is actually crucially strong in support of Trench's contentions. (Cameron was in intention completely hostile to Trench.)

I am certain that, just after the murder, Lambie did run to Miss Birrell's house and identify the man who had passed her in the hall as a particular known visitor, a man distantly related to Miss Gilchrist. On her own subsequent testimony to a journalist, the police so scoffed at this that she "allowed herself to be convinced that she had been mistaken". This is a fascinating phrase. Note that she was not convinced by irrefutable evidence having been put before her, but only by "scoffing". If the police had this evidence to hand, why not simply tell her or show her what it was? Was there evidence, but of a kind somehow undivulgeable? Or was there no evidence beyond the conviction of the policemen, based on long years of service? If the latter, then the policemen's convictions should surely be consequent on rather than subsequent to the evidence, and Lambie's identification, on the basis of the mutual familiarity of the parties involved, was harder evidence than anything else which they had to go on before (or, it seems, since).

Let us suppose that the police had good grounds for believing that Lambie's identification was nonsense. (Perhaps the same information that my journalistic informant has. (Or perhaps what he has, to put it another way, is merely what convinced the upper echelons of the force that A.B. was not the murderer. (As far as I can learn, his claim was that he was sitting at home, minding his own business at the time—so it can't be, on this reading, anything so simple as a watertight alibi.)) They thus performed a public duty, and possibly prevented a scandalous miscarriage of justice, by talking her out of it. But, of course, they could hardly straightforwardly admit that that was what had happened. For, at the trial itself, Lambie managed to identify the man as Slater. It would not do to concede that the person whom one of one's leading witnesses was identifying as the murderer, was only her second choice for the part. (Detective Pyper, at the 1914 Enquiry, was clear that Lambie had not mentioned A.B., because he remembered her saying, when he saw her soon afterwards, "that she did not think she would be able to identify the man again". Needless to say, Detective Pyper had not mentioned this at the trial. Well, I mean to say, be fair: no-one asked, did they?)

I have only very little difficulty in believing that the leading lights of the Glasgow C.I.D. deliberately suborned the witnesses into suppressing all mention of the A.B. affair. This would not have been hard to arrange, one imagines, for I cannot easily see how any of them could gain by the truth being known (after all, the whole scandal had been providentially dumped onto the unlucky Slater)—whereas I can easily see how they would suffer from the displeasure of the Glasgow police force, if they chose to be independent-minded, and drag the name of a perfectly innocent man through the mud. "I am astonished to hear such a statement made, and I say quite solemnly it is not true," said Ord, lover of truth—which is slightly surprising all the same, for if Cameron had heard of it at the time, you would think some mention of it would somehow have filtered up through the ranks, and so be a little less astonishing. (At times like this, one should keep in mind what happened to Trench and Cook. They were ruined, and perhaps even harried into early graves, because they wished to see justice done to a man of absolutely no account to them, except that he had been imprisoned unfairly. And either they were lying, or people like Ord and Orr (another high-ranking official, whose confusingly similar name makes him difficult to "see" properly) were lying.)

(Truly, if you were a witness, and your local chief-constable leaned on you, what would you do? We might note that Trench never found out exactly what transpired on the first visit of the police to Miss Birrell's house, when they were headed by no less a person than Douglas, the Chief Constable. Neither, to the best of my knowledge, has anyone else since. I cannot rid myself of the feeling that a clever man with a head start could outsmart all of these prestigious officials.)

Twenty-One

On the reading that I adhere to, the murder was accidental. Some business associate, or, more probably, some relative called in, fully aware that the servant-girl Lambie would soon be back. He threatened her, not for the first time perhaps, but on this occasion he possibly stepped up the pressure a little, and actually struck her. Either he overestimated her ability to absorb a blow, or he caught her off balance, and she was knocked down. Or perhaps something like that was merely in the back of his mind, but, whatever was going on, he can hardly have expected her to knock her head heavily on the coal-settle as she fell over.

(I must confess I cannot quite fit the three knocks into the scheme of things. It seems to me that, if she cracked her skull forcibly against the scuttle (which was displaced, and the lid of which was actually broken) she cannot possibly have given the knocks. The point is made that her right arm was extended, but, even so, are we to believe she struck the floor three times while lying on her back?

Let us listen to Adams' evidence in chief. "About 7 o'clock, I was sitting in the dining-room with my two sisters, Laura and Rowena. When I was sitting there I heard a sound like a thud, and three distinct knocks, as if wanting assistance, up above in Miss Gilchrist's dining-room. My sister Laura drew my attention to it." Now, in view of my previously expressed confidence as to the veracity of Adams, I am rather embarrassed to have to say that I wonder about this. If he heard "a sound like a thud, and three distinct knocks", his attention must already have been on it, without needing his sister Laura's assistance. This is fairly trivial, but I also remember reading several contemporary newspaper reports on the day or so after the murder, all of which state that Adams was actually in another room at the time, and heard nothing. And his sister came into the room where he was and expressed concern about events upstairs, in somewhat less precise terms than this. Quite possibly all this is as Adams phrased it above, but I must say I suspect that much post factum reconstruction is going on here, and that there were no three clear knocks. (Reports of a *separate* noise before a fall are pretty constant however, and it is never a shout. I'm not sure what it was. Two parts of the same fall? The scuttle? A chair being fallen against? The actual striking?)

The cause of her estrangement from her relatives was the division of her father's will, from which she had benefitted disproportionately. This is well attested. I think it is not going too far to state that such causes of dissension among close members of a family (and particularly so if they are near neighbours) remain live issues, as such circumstances always give rise to opportunities for the wounds to be picked over. At about this time, Miss Gilchrist (whom any relative could with some legitimacy think of as being someone who had deprived him or her of their proper portion) was busy with her own will. In this there were numerous small legacies, but the bulk of the estate went to the family of an ex-servant of hers, a Mrs Ferguson, one of whose daughters was called Marion Gilchrist Ferguson. In November 1908, a codicil, if I remember correctly, shifted the weight further towards the daughters, from the mother. In other words (be the technicalities what they might): those who stood to ays with the Fergusons) to be a surrogate family—that, at least, forced her out to other people. (There were persistent rumours that Mrs Ferguson was in fact Miss Gilchrist's illegitimate daughter. (This rumour seems to have attached itself to almost every female in the case, but the most popular available discussion of the Slater case treats this as a known fact!) I take them all to be malicious invention, attempting to interpret the previously mentioned facts as sensationally as possible. I see no reason to believe them. (In the end, from the point of view of the crime, it probably doesn't even matter whether any of the numerous rumours of this type are true or not.)

It is easy, perhaps too easy, to imagine what effect this news would have on someone who might reasonably have expected to be a major beneficiary (or one of the eventual beneficiaries), and thus at last receive money which, in a sense, was already theirs, but out on a sort of extended loan. (Presumably, it would have been something of a consolation to them to think that, although Marion Gilchrist had *their* money, there was really no-one she could possibly give it to. She had no other family. Eventually it had to come back.) To go no further: it would have been no surprise if some sort of representations had been made on the subject. (For the will is, in fact, surely a little odd, and glacially severe to her own family. Perhaps she was deliberately punishing her relatives for their coldness towards her?) Indeed, perhaps a letter had been written to her by someone, expressing this view in less than temperate tones.

To describe the deceased, as the Lord Advocate did, as having not a single enemy in the world, is to pay perhaps too great a tribute to the fortitude of the overlooked legatees. (Incidentally, the Lord Advocate seemed struck by the smallness of Miss Gilchrist's house. He made a particular point of commenting on it. I suspect that someone who takes a house of six rooms, with hallway, lobbies, etc., to be noteworthily small, is out of touch with more than psychological reality.)

(I learned from my mother, whom I visited on the coast during the last few days, that, as a message-girl in the 1930s, she herself worked hours substantially the same as Mary Barrowman. She also knew next to nothing of the case, which is rather piquant, considering that, at the time she lived in West Princes Street, reading crime thrillers was one of her major hobbies. (I remember more than once going down the street to buy one for her absolutely at random from the stock of a nearby General Store in West Graham Street.) (I have also learned that the point about the Watcher's accent was indeed elicited from the witness Annie Rankin M'Haffie by the trial judge, but it is possible he pre-empted the defence counsel.)

Twenty-Two

I suppose West Princes Street nowadays is not quite as impressively quiet as it was just before the First World War, but it remains, as I imagine it always was, a street which it is impossible even to conceive of as crowded, except under very abnormal circumstances. I cannot remember that there was ever a crowd in it when I lived there. Since then, the Scottish Ballet has taken up residence in a former Territorial Army Drill Hall, so I suppose there are occasionally parking problems thereabouts. (The building is on the left, as one runs down towards Woodlands Drive, the next intersection.) Doubtless some member of the Royal Family formally opened it, in which case there will probably have been a modest crowd there, gazing wide-eyed at such supernatural entities moving freely among us.

I do remember once running out of my close-mouth, hurrying down the stairway, and turning right. It was already very dark, and presumably winter. I suppose I was in my early teens, and going to something like a boy-scout meeting in the Church Hall in Garnethill. (It still exists, although at least the first part of all the roads which I might have taken leading to it have gone, fallen into the deep valley of a motorway.) I immediately saw four or five youths, only slightly older than myself, coming towards me, and I dropped out onto the road as I passed them. As I did so, one of them called out to me, "Hey, Mister!" (which adult address was immensely flattering, even though it was dark, and I was, as I think I remember, wearing a long coat). He then pointed to another member of the happy throng, and added a phrase which graphically indicated that this other youth had at some time had sexual intercourse with a black woman. I heard the corroboratory phrase, "Aye, I rode her twice, and I got nothing out of her", drift towards me on the mysterious air, as I gratefully disappeared beyond them, with a forced smile, proud that I was now getting to the point when I could be mistaken for an adult, with all its attendant joys. (This is a mistake which many people now make on a more or less regular basis.)

Even so, this apparition was not of a crowd. And I wonder if, indeed, there ever was a great crowd in that small, circumscribed area of the city since the day or so after the murder, when the pavements were at times apparently impassable. At at least one point, a policeman had to move sightseers along, to clear a path. I had, needless to say, no sense of that crowd ever having been there on any of the numerous times that I walked over that spot.

It is strange that a few moments' manipulation of a chair should convert so unremarkable a pair of windows into an item of legitimate mass curiosity. And, as it is a fairly widely accepted contention, that a murderer is drawn back to the scene of the crime, it is not unreasonable to suppose that there mingled with the innocent, if perhaps somewhat ghoulish bystanders, perhaps once, perhaps twice, a person who had some considerable familiarity with the mysterious zone behind those tantalizing windows, and who, one might say, was ultimately the reason why all the others were there.

There was, however, another certain visitor of great interest there once, although he came at a less public, less well-attended hour. To wit: "I am informed that Rattman says that a few nights after the murder he referred to it, and that I (Slater) had said I had not heard of it. This must be a mistake. I remember we were standing near my house about midnight on one occasion, and what I certainly meant was that I had not known that the scene of the murder was so near at hand. We then went to have a look at the street where it took place."

Of all the strange juxtapositions which this affair threw up, I think this must be just about the strangest. It seems to me that this moment rivals even the murderer (if such it was) walking out past Lambie and Adams. This is probably the second or third night after the killing. (The body has perhaps that day been removed.) One imagines that the street, at such a time, reposes in its habitual calm. Round the corner walk two visitors to the city, naturally curious at the coincidence of a murder while they happen to be so nearby. (Rattman is on the quickest route home to his own lodgings in Cromwell Street. (I know a young woman who lives in Cromwell Street. In fact, she signalled to me yesterday, at Charing Cross (one minute away from Slater's house), from behind her bicycle.))

They walk up the street, and stop more or less at the right place, looking up at more or less the correct windows. They do it, as little worried by guilt as we are now. One of them has a pawn-ticket for a brooch in one of his pockets. Lambie is elsewhere, perhaps sleeping, perhaps trying to sleep. Adams is no doubt in his own house, a few steps away from where the two Germans stand, looking nonchalantly upwards, hoping to derive a little more from their scrutiny. Perhaps he is sleeping too. His sisters are no doubt also there, one of whom will identify Slater positively, although she can hardly have seen him before. If she were to go over to her bedroom window now, and lift the curtain aside, she would probably see only an empty garden—a few walls, a few back windows, perhaps some in which the lights were still blazing, (I remember how often my mother was astonished, looking over in the morning to the back of Grant Street, where many lights had obviously been left on all night, and were now wanly burning on into the bright return of day. She could not understand this. But I, who now live in a rented room where the electricity for lighting is paid for by the landlord, I understand it all too well)—yet it is always, I suppose, possible that she has a bedroom overlooking the street; and, if so, for a minute or two, she might really see Slater.

Let us suppose a man were now to run out of that fatal stairway, perhaps before bustling off to the left with a confederate, or to the right, to go to the Church Hall in Garnethill. But, seeing Rattman and Slater, he stops, and good-humouredly goes over towards them, and engages them in pleasant conversation, perhaps about jewel robbery, or the validity of the Not Proven verdict. They laugh quietly, as suits the occasion, and, just before he disappears, he mentions to Slater that he will spend almost all of the next twenty years in custody for the murder of that old lady who used to live up there. What an outburst of disbelieving guttural laughter floods into of the calmness of the night! Perhaps Mr. Adams awakens in a sweat. The footsteps recede, and are replaced by other footsteps.

Twenty-Three

This may merely be my exhaustion or ignorance or boredom speaking through me, but I feel that I have by now at least touched on most of the points of the case. This, in other words, is the right moment for at last revealing to the world the identity of the real killer. Unfortunately, I have no-one to suggest, beyond remarking that A.B. has a lot of explaining to do (or ought to have had (and perhaps did)), as also would any of the other nephews or relations who could be mistaken for him. (I have not written about the case for over a week. However, I did describe it as best I could a few days ago to some people I was visiting, and one of them, on being told as many of the relevant facts as I could summon up, instantly suggested the possibility that perhaps Lambie had had an affair with A.B., and thus identified him out of sheer mischief. (The theory then goes that the police, knowing of this, would see fit to discount her evidence.) I don't believe this for a single moment, but it is annoying to realise that this ingenious possibility had not even so much as occurred to me. It suggests all too clearly infinite other possibilities that I have failed even to glimpse. (One might weaken the premise to, that Lambie had some, unknown, reason for wishing to get even with A.B. But even so—sufficient to accuse him of murder within 15 minutes of the crime? Of course, it's just *possible* (perhaps protecting the man whom she recognised, by throwing the blame from him, onto A.B.), but it has been a wonderfully well-kept, rumour-free secret, and I cannot help but feel that the giant invisible rabbits are not too far away, if we start to countenance suggestions like this. But who knows?

And a couple of days ago, I was talking to my landlady's agent—a likeable sexagenarian from (I think) Wester Ross, whom I have known and chatted to for several years—in the large front room of the house, which he is at present decorating. During our wide-ranging, witty, intelligent and literate discussion, I asked him if he had heard of the Slater case. "Slater?", he asked. "Old Oscar? I knew Oscar Slater." (Both had married members of the Italian community in Scotland, and this shared interest caused their paths to cross.) "He was a very bitter man. A very bitter man." It seemed to me from his manner than he was definitely reluctant to discuss this further. I said, "You can"t blame him for that, can you?" His reply to this was something along the lines of, "He was a dealer in white slavery, and a fence; the solicitor who helped him got nothing. The policeman who got kicked out because of him got nothing." There was such an uncomfortable, living hostility at work here, that I let the matter drop for a while. But I discover that I have been having my rent collected, month by month, for years, (sometimes a few days late, I must admit: occasionally his fault, more usually mine), by a man who knew Oscar Slater. (Later on, when I returned to the subject, I did learn that he had not thought badly of Slater at the time—he seemed to be a quiet, polite, inoffensive man—but that later, as he had learned more about the case, he had turned against him. (It seems to me, perhaps fancifully, that I can hear in this episode a confused echo of the process (well, even if he technically didn't do it, he is such an unsavoury character that we might as well put him inside and save society the trouble later) by which Slater was finally found guilty by nine members of the jury.)

Twenty-Four

I have come reluctantly to the conclusion that my interest in the Slater case threatens to founder utterly on the almost inevitable rocks of that ambition which challenges just about everyone who deals with an unsolved real-life murder mystery—to wit, the need to resolve the affair definitively once and for all. I simply cannot do this. Furthermore, I cannot rid myself of the (doubtless unfounded) conviction that I have at least touched on the main points of the case, which all the more stymies my impulse for large-scale endeavour. I fear that, if I am to go on at all (even if my major drive is to get as much mileage as possible out of the notes I have made) the only course of action that greatly appeals to me is to pick off my notes more or less piecemeal, one at a time. With luck, this may take me so long that new developments arise, as a result of which the case can be triumphantly solved.

But, before embarking on this sadly inferior mode of operation, I will sign off the heroic phase of my quest by describing something of little or no interest which happened the Saturday before last, 11 days ago. I was walking into town, taking the opportunity to pass the scene of the crime yet again. When I was still some 15 or 20 seconds short of the fatal doorway, I noticed an old man exit from it, and go down the five or six (modern-tiled) steps to the main road. This was in itself unusual, for I believe there is only one domestically inhabited flat in that closeway. (The murder flat is obviously part of a widespread refurbished complex, internally linked to its lower neighbours in a manner I have not even begun to try to fathom.)

The man was broad-shouldered, somewhat taller (I would think) than myself, his inconsidered pursuant, and aged 70 or so. At the first gap in the parked cars, he stepped off the pavement, and crossed to the far side of the road. A middle-aged woman was standing by the door of one of the pair of parked cars which he reached the other side of the road by bisecting—which he had, in effect, passed on his way towards St. George's Road. He obviously knew her, for he stopped, turned round to face the road, and addressed her parallel to his right shoulder. I had by now, of course, very nearly made up my 15 to 20 seconds of leeway, and I looked across at the old man as I passed.

Every six months or so I see someone who has the sort of unusual, East European, slightly *Politburo* look that reminds me of my father.

It is a visual type which is not, one may say, indigenous to these surroundings. Not only was this man my six-monthly revenant, but he was a remarkably high-class example of the genus. In fact, my view lingered on him for so long (with some awkwardness, given that I was by then almost past him, across the road)—impressed by his first-rate ability as a mime, that *he* looked across at *me,* perhaps resentful of my gaze.

I suppose it is just, just possible that he was alive at the time of the murder. Of course, I could not identify him with certainty, if I met him in another place. Of course, I would identify him with certainty if I once more saw an old man pass down those stairs in front of me, who reminded me powerfully of my father. And, of course, that could be his brother. I think my father is in Germany at the moment, to comfort one of my uncles over the impending loss of his wife, who has been ill for months (hospitalized before I even started writing any of this), but I am not entirely sure.

Twenty-Five

The whole question of the second man is a fascinating one. I believe, at the moment at least, that the two men whom Agnes Brown saw running away (for I still believe she was there, and did see two men running away) included the man who walked out past Lambie and Adams. (One must believe something. Perhaps someone youngish, in a grey coat, with a flat cap, did just happen to be running down that street within minutes of someone else, youngish, in a grey coat, with a flat cap, walking out of the house in question, and haring down the stairs; but why go looking for trouble?) If so, the question is: where and how did he link up with his companion?

It seems to me that the suggestion that this second person may have been hiding on the unoccupied floor above (perhaps after having left the house between Adams's two visits (and perhaps being the actual murderer—the man who walked past being merely an accomplice of some sort, if only after the fact)) is rather a wild one. (Apart from anything else, as I have already said, the area is narrow yet exposed, and does not feel like a shelter.) Besides which, it requires the further supposition (well, it usually does—perhaps some people can believe he stayed up there for a more of less indefinite period (perhaps the old man I saw a few days ago emerging was the murderer at last making his escape?)) that the man ran downstairs more or less immediately after he saw (or heard—could he see?—I doubt it very much) A.B. run away. This is obviously absurd, as Adams was still at the door. And if we wait until Adams goes into the house, this gives A.B. a few highly interesting seconds on the street outside, when he presumably wastes a little time by running on the spot. And, anyway, would Adams and/or Lambie not hear a man running downstairs two open doors away, during (presumably) an appalled silence? (Of course, they might hear it, but not register it under the circumstances; but even this is pretty desperate.)

We may as well make use here of the evidence, in detail highly untrustworthy, but in sheer weight suggestive, to the effect that someone was, in those days, given to hanging around the pavement thereabouts, or, more impressively, was met by the houseowners in the close-mouth and stairway of No. 46 West Princes Street, very nearly immediately opposite, on more than one occasion, suspiciously gauche and uncommunicative, trying to make himself inconspicuous with spectacular lack of success (or, presumably, practice). In short, someone was waiting at the street for his companion's descent, which he expected, although it is far from likely that he expected him to be moving at quite such speed.

Twenty-Six

The behaviour of the witnesses as to identification of the Watcher at times rises to high comedy. ("When you spoke of a longish neck, did you mean something longer than the average?"—"No.") Reading their testimony, one feels very keenly the force of the suggestion that the verdict of the jury was, in the light of the evidence, perverse. (For an appeal to be allowed because of such a plea (that the verdict was simply inconsistent with the evidence) is next door to unheard-of (I believe it did happen in England, *once*). Usually, sage and possibly incontrovertible remarks are made to the effect that the jury had the inestimable advantage of actually being there, and seeing the expressions on all the faces (as if those who could miss the force of a crucial suggestion could not also misread the expression on a face), and that extreme caution must be taken before their decision be overturned by those who must rely purely on written evidence and submissions. This is all true, of course but I think we can say that, if a Court of Appeal can hold that the Slater case is one in which it is not possible to say that the jury reached a verdict *despite* the evidence rather than because of it, then this heading of appeal will be of such limited practical use as to be completely superfluous.)

One of the Watcher witnesses, observing a man on the area bridge of No. 46 a few days before the murder (that is, on the flat extension of stonework between the steps and the doorway to the close proper), put up a wonderful display of obstinacy as he sought to mitigate the fact that his wife had been with him at the time and yet did not remember either seeing the man when the husband drew her attention to him, or, indeed, even hear her husband make such a remark. I suspect he did see someone there, but his refusal to make the slightest obeisance to a reasonable objection was instructive.

(Apparently what he said was something to the effect that, "He looks as if he is watching for a ladylove". It gave me a nasty shock to read this, for, of course, the reason why such a swain would ardently observe Miss Gilchrist's flat could surely only be Helen Lambie. Lambie's innocence of the actual crime in all its circumstances was threatened by this, and I realised that she might in some sense have been a party to the intrusion, which is a further complication that I can do without, and had previously hardly so much as considered. I remember that M. L. had once given me a lift three-quarters of the way home, and that as we passed the site of the now

91

vanished newspaper shop, he said, with significant emphasis, "It took her a long time to get a paper, didn't it?" Actually, I don't think ten minutes is excessive, but I felt *[quite wrongly, apparently]* that I was being offered a hint, obviously bearing on Lambie's complicity in the crime or otherwise, and this slightly perturbed me, as I could make nothing of it.

(Perhaps I should insert here a couple of William Park's remarks in this connection, to wit: "None of them [i.e. the Watcher witnesses] had beforehand spoken of any such man, or had reported his presence to the Constable on street patrol." This is true, but not, I think, final. Much happens which does not get reported to the police. (And a certain amount does not happen, which does.) And, from the same source: "The whole of this 'Loiterers' evidence we should have no hesitation in dismissing as worthless, nay, dangerous." One need only recall that all these people were prepared to swear to Slater to see the force of this. But I must say that I am sufficiently impressed by the sheer volume of this evidence to believe that, shortly before the murder, someone was indeed hanging about opposite that part of the street where Miss Gilchrist (and the Adams) stayed, in a singularly inexpert manner. It seems to me that there *is* something here which needs to be explained, rather than dismissed out of hand as nothing more than the inevitable concomitant of a spectacular murder. So many different, separate sources are involved that I cannot brush it aside easily as a mere permutation of inventions and innocent bystanders.))

Twenty-Seven

Of course, the only convincing witness to identity was MacBrayne, "the man from the big shop on Sauchiehall Street" (Slater's words on seeing him in the police station), who saw Slater standing outside his house in Saint George's Road at about 8.15 on the night of the killing, while he himself was returning from work. That it was indeed the Monday night was fixed in his mind, he averred, by the fact that, at about that time he had also noticed a passing ambulance wagon, which had caused him to think that it was going to the house of the murdered woman. (I have not seen it discussed anywhere, but I assume that it was, in fact, going somewhere else. The body was, I think, left in situ over night. Perhaps someone else had just died, in a way deemed less memorable. (Note that MacBrayne had already heard of the murder. No doubt some visitor to the large, centrally situated shop had reported the striking news (already an objectified event while the murderer's pulse had still to return to normal) to one of the staff. (In this MacBrayne had the advantage of Slater, who had eaten a routine meal, and had made some more routine plans.)))

MacBrayne's identification, of course, testifying to a moment over an hour later than the lifting and setting down of a fine heavy neighbourhood chair, was not in any way conclusive of Slater's innocence, as such. If Slater had carried out the murder with the callousness that the Lord Advocate insisted he did, then there would be nothing much odd in his standing unconcerned outside his house an hour and a minute afterwards. However, the Prosecution, eager to enlist the attractive ticket-collector, Annie Armour, in its case, was committed to the theory that the murderer—or Slater, as he was called, to protect the guilty—had fled, conscience-stricken (conscience-stricken?) to the outer suburbs, thence to make his chastened and horrorstruck way homewards, still carrying the hammer.

This point was overlooked, it seems, by the five judges of the Appeal, who dismissed the MacBrayne episode as "immaterial". The idea that an item of evidence which will effectively *disprove* the prosecution case if accepted is immaterial to a review of the justice of the proceedings, and can be dismissed prima facie, is surely an interesting contribution by the Scottish Judiciary to legal theory in general. But, whatever the later opinion of this fine body of forensic brains turned out to be, it might be thought that the Defence at the trial would have been grateful for MacBrayne's deposition to have been made available to them. And, as Park remarks, MacBrayne had gone voluntarily to the police. It was up to them, if they didn't want his evidence, to send him to the agent for the prisoner.

Curiously enough, however, his evidence did not reach the panel's agents. It is all so very strange. Superintendent Ord said that he had sent it on, and that, in effect, it must have got lost in transit. Well, *of course*. That explains it. (A passing pickpocket, perhaps?) This is all technically possible, I dare say, but I don't know quite why— whenever Ord assures one of something, I tend to suspect that the opposite might well be the case. I incline strongly to the belief that the police deliberately suppressed this item of information, as part of a wider campaign to ensure that Slater did not somehow manage to wriggle out of getting his just deserts, simply because so many facts happened, most unreasonably, to favour him. (Slater, however, was given to claiming that he had been "framed" (sic) by the Glasgow Police. I take this to mean that he thought that those responsible for the prosecution knew perfectly well he was not guilty, but wanted him condemned for reasons of their own. Personally, I still doubt this. But it would be interesting to know what interpretation Ord, for instance, put on MacBrayne's evidence. To suppose that he simply did not believe it is to give him the benefit of considerable doubts—and why *should* we suppose that anyway?)

For, note this: Park points out that the Prosecution must have been certain that the Defence had not found MacBrayne independently, or they would not have put forward Annie Armour, the ticket-girl, to give out drastically vulnerable evidence. (This, Park adds, "is a circumstance which makes his (MacBrayne's) suppression almost a criminal act". (Actually, I see no need now for that circumspect "almost". If this is not seeking to pervert the course of justice, then it is difficult to know what is.)) It must be said that, if MacBrayne's deposition had reached the Lord Advocate, then a legal innocent might well think that he lied at that point of his closing address when he claimed that "nothing further is known of his movements" after the murder, until Slater turned up at 9.30 "gasping and panting for money" at the entrance of the Motor Club, from the Sloper Club next door, where he had gone to play at cards that fatal evening, but had experienced a bad run. (The beginning of a very bad run indeed.)

(It might seem uncalled for to assume that so august a gentleman as the Lord Advocate was lying here, were it not highly likely that he had already lied during his final address, which is to say, at the celebrated conclusion to his opening remarks, to the effect that he would show later on how Slater had come to know that Miss

94

Gilchrist was possessed of jewelry. No evidence whatever of this had been led during the trial, and the Lord Advocate never returned to the subject. Now, with the best will in the world, what explanation is more likely than that this was, to use a layman's term, deliberate deceit? Indeed, it is hard to imagine innocent explanations that are at all plausible. I repeat, absolutely no such evidence had been led. (After all, how could it? No such evidence existed.) Are we to suppose that the Lord Advocate did not know this, or that he had somehow forgotten it? The remainder of the address is sufficient to show that, although possessed of a fine imagination (*"gasping* and *panting* for money"* is pure—what is the word?—pure invention on his part), the man is not given to confusion of mind. He seems to have been one of those deeply undesirable practitioners (a sort of legal version of Ord, perhaps) who feel that short-comings in the evidence are to be supplemented by rhetoric and flights of fancy—which to him seem to have at least equal weight with proven facts—and that justice is merely another name for winning his cases at all costs.

(However, by all means let us at least assume in his favour that the Lord Advocate had not heard of MacBrayne either. It is, I think, perfectly possible. This is a case in which the police felt it necessary to share all it knew with as few people as possible, and only those who could be *absolutely trusted*.)

Twenty-Eight

I discover I have noted down a few more excerpts from this famous final address of the Prosecution, and I may as well treat them here:

(i) One of my favourites: "You are quite safe to assume that there is no case of mistaken identity here". Of course. Hardly needed to be said, did it? The witness had a clear view of the back of his head across the street late at night. The witness did not notice a foreign accent. The witness was not sure at the time, but has been thinking it over, and now, three months later, thinks it was certainly him. Good God—what more could you want? (If the Lord Advocate was here addressing himself solely to the testimony of Lambie, Adams, and Barrowman—I quote out of context, from brief notes—I withdraw the previous remarks, and ask you to discount them.)

(ii) "Now, the motive for this crime is as plain as daylight." He means jewel theft. Of course, he could be right, though most would doubt it, and his more detailed theory is so absurd that it could be as plain as daylight only to someone already blinded. On the Lord Advocate's view, we have here a callous jewel-thief, so expert that he cases his victim by standing for long periods on the pavement outside the house in question, gazing up at the windows, making himself obvious to all and sundry. Having thus familiarized himself with the habits of the household, he puts his knowledge to good use by effecting entry (it is never stated how) during a ten minute absence of the maid, whom he presumably has learnt has two half-days off, when the old lady is left quite alone. (Perhaps he relishes a challenge?) Once inside, in the approved manner of the professional thief, he spends most of his time kneeling on the old lady's prone body, beating her head in with a hammer (which he subsequently cannot bear to part with, and carries with him to America). To round off a satisfying and professional evening's work, he goes into the back bedroom, scatters a few papers over the floor, leaves behind him an incriminating box of matches complete with single spent example thereof, and pockets one item of valuable jewelry from a dish holding four or five such items, the rest of which he ignores. Perhaps he is so tired by his exertions that he does not wish to be weighed down by too heavy a load. ("The murder was coolly and deliberately planned and executed by no bungler, but by a daring, cold-blooded, expert performer.")

(iii) "He was a man who was certainly in possession of a weapon

96

with which admittedly the deed could be done." Which is to say, an ordinary light household hammer, fit for knocking nails into ordinary walls, on five continents. Were there many men in Scotland who were *not* "certainly in possession of a weapon with which admittedly the deed could be done"? Are we to believe that a search of the Lord Advocate's own august premises would not yield such a weapon?

(iv) "This old lady. . . living in a respectable house, though no doubt a comparatively small house. . ." This seems to mean, compared to the Lord Advocate's house. I suspect most of the witnesses would find Miss Gilchrist's house distinctly more spacious than their own.

(v) We have already dealt with the "gasping and panting". Slater turned up at the gambling club next door to the one he was at late on the night of the murder (one seems to have been an offshoot of the other), looking for ready cash, and offering to give Henderson, the Clubmaster of the Motor Club, a cheque for whatever cash in hand he might be able to give him. I do not know the etiquette of gambling clubs, but Slater insisted that this was a normal way of raising money in a local crisis, and I don't see why we shouldn't believe him. But the Lord Advocate made the quite gratuitous addition, "I dare say you have your own ideas as to whether that cheque would have been honoured." What is this if not the quite unfounded suggestion that it would not have been so honoured, and, as such, was surely a suggestion that the Lord Advocate had no right whatever to make. No evidence was ever led, as far as I remember, to the effect that Slater dishonoured his debts, or passed bad cheques. (In fact, Slater showed a curious punctiliousness about money. He believed in banking etc. as much as any bourgeois.) But, of course, the Lord Advocate never actually said so in so many words, did he, that Slater would dishonour his debt. Advanced legal technique.

(vi) "He may be, and probably is, the worst of men, but he is entitled to as fair a trial as if he was the best of men. [Very true. Very laudable. And, of course, where such remarks are made, are they not in themselves almost a guarantee of fairness. But I interrupt.] He may be one of the most degraded of mortals [as who *may* not?], he may be a cheat [evidence?], he may be a robber [evidence?], a burglar [evidence?], or the worst of characters ("I had it that the man, like a great number of those who came to Glasgow (this "great number" was never heard of again) lived etc. etc.), but that does not infer (sic—perhaps a legal use? (for "allow us to infer": or perhaps the Lord Advocate actually means "imply")) that he committed murder." This whole tirade reminds me of that old ploy so beloved of some philosophers, the trick of asking someone not to think of a rhinoceros. What is this actually saying, if not that Slater *is* in fact the worst, the most degraded of mortals, a cheat, a robber, a burglar, and the worst of characters; but, hold on—he may not actually have done it. It would seem to me to be somewhat more surprising if such a man *hadn't* done it. If only to fill the gap in his experience. After all, he seems to have done everthing else.

(vii) Returning diligently to the library to check up a previous point (*evidently point (i) above,*), I learn that the remark of the Lord Advocate was not specifically tied to the star witnesses, although the very next remark he makes is, "The prisoner is hopelessly unable to produce a single witness who saw that he was anywhere else than at the scene of the murder that night," which suggests that his mind might be running along those lines.

This observation is, of course, a trifle unfair on Slater's mistress, and the latter's lady's maid, both of whom were quite clear that he was at home at that time. The Lord Advocate may not have believed them, but it might have been fairer to acknowledge their mere existence at least, rather than to risk misleading the jury by suggesting that they were not there and that no-one had ever heard them speak. (The Lord Advocate, by the way, did not cross-examine Mlle Antoine, merely saying, "I have no questions to ask"—giving it, as he did so, according to at least one newspaper, a distinct emphasis. Perhaps he simply did not see her?)

It might be thought that Slater's mistress would testify in his favour through hell and high water, but, even so, that would leave the maid, Schmalz. Here too, a certain loyalty would not have been unprecedented, but it could hardly be taken for granted all the same, and, besides, Schmalz had actually been handed her notice by Slater on the day of the crime! ("I'm afraid I'm going to have to dismiss you, Catherine—I'm going to kill a litle old lady, hang around long enough to arouse suspicion, and then emigrate.") It seems to me that this would, if anything, be an argument for revenge rather than loyalty. At all events, are we to believe it is something which the Lord Advocate simply *overlooked*?

Twenty-Nine

William Roughead, the great criminologist, claimed to possess a photograph (and I don't doubt for a moment that he did) of the chair with which the old lady was most probably battered to death, perhaps within two minutes of being unconcernedly (or otherwise) seated on top of it. It quite clearly showed, he said, the bloody imprint of a right hand, holding the chair from behind. He remarked what a pity it was that at that time the Glasgow police did not use fingerprinting in their attempts to solve crimes. (With such unerring intuitive gifts as theirs, did they need it?) Whatever his exact words may have been, I was left with the definite impression that finger-printing had not yet been invented, for if it had, the case would surely have been solved within hours.

Now, there is something distinctly strange about all this. I am faced with a stray note taken from, presumably, a book on the case, which states baldly: "From 1899 to 1906, 192 prisoners were iden-tified by fingerprints." I presume this means, in Glasgow. (Perhaps it refers to Scotland.) I certainly recall reading in the contemporary newspapers remarks which made it clear that fingerprinting was, from the outset, a live possibility. So, what happened?

Were fingerprints taken from the flat? I have heard nothing to suggest that they were. I have heard nothing to suggest, for instance, that Slater was ever fingerprinted. But if fingerprinting was available, and yet was not used, the reason for the why not requires some explanation. (Pure incompetence seems, once again, the favourite. (And, of course, if fingerprinting was carried out, what was found? (But presumably it was not.))) Given the circumstances—the box of matches, the opened document-case, the absence of other leads—fingerprinting would seem to be a very obvious resource.

(By the way, according to Detective Inspector Pyper's evidence at the trial, "Douglas [the Chief Constable] took away the box of matches and [the] used match." (It was at Pyper's own instigation, on the evening of the murder, that Lambie, checking through the old lady's appurtencances, discovered that the brooch was missing.)

(A propos the Chief Constable himself: "I have been ringing up Douglas, and he is convinced that A.B. had nothing to do with it," Ord said to Trench, while the latter, I think, was making out his report on his visit to Miss Birrells's. Truly, Douglas is, as I may have said before, not far away from being the key to all this. *He* visited

A.B. on the day after the murder, and *he* called off the bloodhounds thereafter. Trench never heard a word of what happened at that vital meeting, despite numerous attempts—not a word. This is surely rather odd.

And yet, Douglas is a completely shadowy figure to students of the case. I have never so much as seen a photograph of him. He was not called at the trial. I know next to nothing about him. Even so, I am convinced that he knew the answer to most of the largest, most puzzling questions in this whole affair.

(I cannot prevent myself from adding here that my family's telephone number in 37 West Princes Street, in the old-fashioned, named exchange system, was *Douglas* 4343.)))

Thirty

I have discovered the excerpt from, I think, the Glasgow News, which has a particular bearing on the three knocks, and where exactly the Adams' family was at the time of the crime. To wit, (Adams is speaking): "About 7 o'clock, or to be precise, for I looked at the clock, at three minutes past seven, one of my sisters came to me while I was sitting in the dining-room, and in an anxious tone said, 'I think Miss Gilchrist has fallen down. There was a fearful thud.' Possibly this is just another reporter getting it wrong, but it is is not without interest. I may as well continue, and pick off a few more excerpts from the contemporary reports of this episode. (The Evening News was, I think, the one of the three available Glasgow evening papers that Miss Gilchrist bought, or had bought for her. It went out of business many hundreds of thousands of copies later.)

"A little later, however, several rapid knocks on the floor overhead were heard, and her brother went upstairs again." I must confess, to my shame, that I have never quite managed to get clear in my mind which knock was quite which: when the falling stopped; when the murdering stopped; and when the breaking open of the box stopped. Here, it seems that what happened was that the falling brought Adams upstairs. That, once there, he heard the box being opened. (His testimony speaks of him hearing, as he stands at the door for the first time, several sharp repeated sounds, which he took to be the servant-girl, Lambie, breaking up sticks for firewood in the kitchen. He decided that she was not going to answer his knock at the door, but that all was well, and so, thus reassured, he returned downstairs.) And that, once downstairs, he was drawn back up by the sounds of the actual murder. It had not, until this moment, occurred to me that the events might have taken place in this order. It would certainly explain the absence of blood in the bedroom, if the old lady had not yet been attacked, but it is a bit counter-intuitive. On his return upstairs, Adams heard nothing. ("I did not hear any sound the second time" (Trial)). Presumably, by this time, the murderer was already waiting, listening to what was going on outside, and wondering how best to extricate himself from such a situation.

(Of course, the sequence: Fall—Search—Adams—Murder, suggests that it may have been the actual arrival of Adams itself which in some way provoked the murderous assault. But, looked at the other way, is it likely that, after hearing someone ring the doorbell, the visitor would cross back into the dining-room, and beat the prone, fallen body to death? (Presumably the visitor inside would have a fairly good idea of who the outside visitor might be. (On second thoughts: Adams visited so rarely. It *might* have been anyone.))

Perhaps it is unwise to embark on this paragraph, and madness beckons, but here goes. Old ladies do, after all, tend to have fainting fits, and fall to the floor for seemingly inadequate reasons. (By the way, A.B. was a doctor. Who, a tiny and perhaps insane voice asks, would know this better than a doctor?) Now, if one wished to remove from sight a difficult, obstructive and *unnecessary* old lady, how better do it than to simulate a fall? A single well-chosen nudge would surely be enough?

So, one pushes the old lady, and she falls to the ground, hitting her head, as a bonus, heavily against the coal-scuttle. (No. Too lucky. One pushes her, and she falls to the ground. One then lifts her up, and lets her head fall heavily, from some height onto the coal-scuttle. One then returns her body to the floor. That should do, eh? The vindictive old bitch out of the way at last, and no-one else any the worse off for it.)

It is just as well that I am not in the least committed to believing any of this, for the documents suddenly become more difficult. But, anyway, one nips through to get a letter that is vital to one, or perhaps simply would be rather nice to have (might as well pick it up while we are here), with plenty of time (?) still in hand before Lambie returns. The rings on the doorbell, we may be sure, are a horrendous surprise. You wait, blood freezing with horror, etc. There is perhaps half a minute of silence. Presumably, whoever it was has gone away. ("After I had been standing at the door for half a minute or so I heard what I thought was the servant breaking sticks in the kitchen,"—Adams at the trial.) You thus busy yourself with the letters (which, presumably, *are* vital after all.)

Do you know that someone is waiting outside? Do you hear some-one descend the stair? You race through the documents for the letter you want (thus, it must be said, skewering the appearance of normal-ity (which perhaps a broken lid to a case would not do—really, this plan is far from perfect)) and go back to check the old lady's corpse. Good God, she is not dead yet! The whole probably non-existent edifice is beginning to totter. But, whatever else happens, she must not speak. You pick up the chair nearby and hammer her head with the lethally heavy wooden end of one of its legs. There is soon more noise at the door. Enough is enough. Put your coat and hat on (unless, as is more probable, you have never taken them off) and wait. From here the situation largely plays itself. I will walk out past them. What can they do? It is not as if I am an utter intruder. They will not know what is happening, and will not stop me. Then it is my word against the word of whoever it is is there—probably that stupid girl Lambie—and, since I am who I am, I will at least be listened to. What else can I do? Perhaps things will still work out all right. (The sound of breaking sticks seems to follow the ringing at the doorbell. Could it be that—realising that it would no longer be feasible to escape unobserved—oh dear, my pen is running out of ink.

Thirty-One

When Slater first went out again into Sauchiehall Street, after his release, he apparently had great difficulty in recognising it. This is, of course, completely unsurprising. Almost 20 years had passed since he had last seen it. Marion Gilchrist had lived in her West Princes Street house for nearly 30 years. Presumably the Sauchiehall Street she knew latterly was vastly different from the early form of the street.

I find it strange to consider that I have by now been away from West Princes Street for nearly as long a period as that which Slater spent in prison. It is an almost endless expanse of time, of course, but it often seems very little. It would take a dead man not to notice the vast changes that have taken place in the area. Entire streets have disappeared. The familiar layout has been utterly disrupted. It is normal to travel abroad, and return after half a lifetime to discover that the magical backdrops of one's childhood have been crudely and garishly over-painted; but to inhabit continuously the same city, and be subject to more or less random reminders, after a rushed assemblage of far too few years, of the total loss of some of the most treasured venues and landmarks of the private eternity of one's earliest youth, is to find oneself the baffled victim of transience at its most callous.

Yet, a child being brought up there now (not that I ever see any, come to think of it) would have none of these problems. The long line of shops that should still be there, where instead a large car showroom has already stood for so long, contributing so little atmosphere to the street (I remember entering one of these shops, young, on a rainy evening (much rainier than on the night of the murder—it was falling torrentially) with the hood of my duffel-coat up, and, to my immense chagrin, I was mistaken—oh God, the shame of it!—for a girl. (And another shop, outside which a real girl was standing on some other day with one foot resting on her scooter, and with her back to me, reading one of those comics which came out every week, as they did long before and long after. Thinking I recognised her, I stood behind her, reading the comic over her shoulder, though we were roughly the same height. She turned round and favoured me with a look of disdainful perplexity, and, to my astonishment, she was not who I thought she was. (Evidently there is something in that area which favours mistaken identities. I have absolutely no idea who or where she is now.) I remember how desperately I insisted to her that I had thought she was someone else, *really*. This was obviously absurd to her, and she said absolutely nothing in response. (Or the shop of Mr. Hart, the grocer—an Englishman. How, on the day after the Scotland-England football international, when England had (inevitably, unfairly) won, he baited me with the victory, and I responded with such heat that my mother insisted I apologise, although Mr. Hart, if anything, seemed pleased to have scored such a direct hit. ("The Procurator-Fiscal for Lanarkshire (Mr. J. Neil Hart) had an interview today (that is—Dec. 29; the previous brackets were the Glasgow Evening News's own) with Nellie Lambie. . . and with a relative of the murdered lady" Well, well, well. (I suppose this is more probably Miss Burrell than A.B.))))) would not trouble him or her. It would seem an eternally ordered car showroom; just as I have no nostalgia for what was there before those shops.

As to what Miss Gilchrist would make of the "real" West Princes Street—that is to say, the place as it was in the late 1950's and early 1960's—I can only assume she would be horrified by the countless changes for the worse. (Even so, some things would be pleasantly familiar. One of the policemen spoke to seeing Slater loitering in, at, on, or near the chemist's at the foot of the road. This sounds to me suspiciously like that well-known landmark of my youth, MacSween's the Chemist. It closed soon after we left, despite having given the impression of being eternal—for its interior was strangely heavy-wooded, dark, and glowing, and the panels of stonework outside boasted of a lengthy pedigree in a manner utterly suggestive of permanence.

(This edifice is now the store for a Chinese supermarket—the Wah Sang—itself just a block or two up the road, in the direction of Slater's house. I saw as I passed there last evening, a small notice in the doorway of this, which consisted of a battery of Chinese ideographs, which I did not put myself to the trouble of examining closely, interspersed with the words "Falkirk" and "Johnstone". (Both of these towns are moderately near Glasgow, but, to the best of my knowledge, I have never so much as walked a step in either of them.) I think it is safe to assume that Miss Gilchrist would have, initially at least, horrendous difficulty in assimilating the raison d'être of a change like this, even though one of the minor beneficiaries of her will was, as I remember, a missionary resident in China. (More generally, I myself at times almost believe I am dreaming as I walk through these remnants of the location of my childhood. I have no sense that these are the same old streets. Somehow I feel certain that the same old streets are still in existence elsewhere (in fact, I do often dream about them), and it seems I am actually in quite another part

105

of town.))

This is somewhat similar to a keen sense I have been getting lately—or perhaps I mean it is the exact reverse of it—when walking through the most relevant streets in the area, particularly when deeply embroiled in the case. For the occasional split-second, I will manage to forget what year I am in. (This is perhaps too melodramatic a way of putting it. But it will seem to me that it could just as well be in 1909 or 1985 that I am now where I am, that those windows are lit where they are, and that that pair of people have just passed me. That it could just as well be a day before the murder as a day after, and the old lady could still be up there, alive, as she was for over 10,000 equally real days.)

I suppose it is somewhat macabre that it should take a murder to make me so aware of the realness of history: such things as a photographer's assistant wandering down the same street in 1908, going home for her lunch, as she had so often done (as most of the rest of the large town was doing, more or less—(Debussy! Why should I wonder if Debussy is having a meal now too?)), and seeing somebody awkwardly motionless beside a private, locked, crescent-filling garden, round which no children were running (I suppose) as we did so often in the 1950's. What on earth did they all eat? What did we eat? (Sips thoughtfully at a cup of tea. Decides to stop for the day at this point.)

Thirty-Two

But perhaps I should return to those newspaper reports that I so shamefully ran away from:

(i) "This suggests the possibility that the visitor had some definite purpose in his search." I regret to say that I did not note what "this" was, nor the date of the newspaper. As far as I remember, it referred to the scattered documents, and the suggestion was made in the very first report of the killing. Note also, from a few days later (—if the sequence of notes is anything to go by (which it need not be))

(ii) "They [the police] are now, as has been already stated, MORE THAN SATISFIED [capitalized sub-heading] that the criminal was no professional burglar, and that, in fact, he was known to his victim." From this initial high-point, it seems, from the official point of view, to have been downhill all the way thereafter. We may take this, I think, as the commonsense rank-and-file police view, which was lost sight of in the debacle orchestrated by such as Ord, only to resurface spectacularly with the *affaire Trench*. This newspaper seems to have had at least one reliable source in the police force, for the first mention of Slater (or rather, of the vague, unnamed personage whom we realise, with something of a shock, will in a few days time turn out to be Oscar Slater) comes complete with some very dampening qualifications:

(iii) "but it is to be regretted that the evidence on which the suspicion is based is not of a more substantial nature," and

(iv) "as the evidence tending to show any connection with the G. crime (G. being an abbreviation for either Glasgow or Gilchrist, I forget which) is of the most shadowy nature." (31st December.) This goes to show that at least someone in the know was not losing his head about the brooch clue. In short:

(v) "Whether this effort will lead to a solution of the mystery is, however, doubtful." All too true. I also note a mention of,

(vi) "the usual examination for fingerprints". That insouciant "usual" is most interesting, suggesting that by now that procedure was so normal as to be altogether routine. I have never seen the results of any fingerprint tests mentioned anywhere that I can recall. In short, as the Glasgow Evening News precociously but presciently sums up: "Whatever may be the ultimate solution of the mystery, the West Princes Street tragedy will rank as one of the most important, and, in its early stages at least, one of the most mysterious cases in the criminal annals of Scotland."

Thirty-Three

More notes jotted down at the time from a brief perusal of the newspapers, I'm afraid. (Such of them, at least, as were available to me.)

(i) "She did not think he had got in by the front door, for Miss Gilchrist was always very particular not to open the door when alone." This "she" is presumably Lambie. Needless to say, none of the newspapers, from the first night onwards, breathe a word of the A.B. business. Some sort of protective or censoring process was at work right from the outset. (But, of course, a certain care would be necessary in handling these circumstances. What I mean is, none of the newspapers, rife with speculations as they are, had got wind of any supposed identification by Lambie—or, if they had, they did not so much as whisper of it in print.) But really I should check who the authoress of this statement was, for I do remember that one of the Adams women from downstairs was interviewed and was insistent that the murderer must have climbed up a drain-pipe from the back, a theory subsequently discounted (chiefly from the untouched condition of the windows. (If it was Lambie, of course, then it would somewhat undermine her already shaky credibility—for she can hardly have thought that A.B. came in via the drain-pipe. (Can she?)))

(ii) "The question of how Miss Gilchrist's assailant gained entrance to the house remains the most mysterious point in a case presenting many strange and almost unaccountable features." This point was, nonetheless, never seriously treated at the trial. But remarks like these, made within a day of the murder, show that our reservations as to the value of the legal process are hardly only the comfortable rewards of hindsight.

(iii) The suggestion was at once made that it might have been a stranger who had somehow come into possession of a set of keys. This hit me with some force, for it was a theory which I had never seen so much as mentioned elsewhere, and it certainly had never occurred to me. All this is to get over the question of how a complete stranger could get into a well-guarded house, a situation which now seems to most students of the case to be rather an academic point; but it is certainly worth asking who had keys to the house. I seem to recall reading somewhere that only Miss Gilchrist and Lambie had keys, with a set being kept at Miss Gilchrist's lawyers, but I may merely have dreamed this. (I hesitate to mention that this is not the first time that Miss Gilchrist's lawyers have been brought into this discussion, as I remember they put in a fleeting appearance during the discussion of possible wills.) It is fortunate that Lambie used her keys in front of Adams, for we might otherwise begin to get nervous about where they were. Of course, keys can be copied, but life is too short to consider every possible ramification of the Slater case.

(iv) "Miss Gilchrist, the servant-girl thinks, was wearing a diamond crescent brooch at the time of the murder, and this is said to be missing." I think I have mentioned the possibility that it fell off during the assault, and the murderer picked it up, more from a reflex desire to impose neatness than anything else. The body does seem to have been rearranged, for (according, I think, to Pyper) the left leg was crossed over the right, below the knees, which is hardly an attitude one would naturally fall into. Notice this bloody brooch. It won't stay still. 'Tis here—'tis here—'tis gone. But who has it? Where was it, on the morning of December the 22nd 1908 (the day after the murder)? At the bottom of the river? In someone's pocket? Being worn on someone else's blouse? (God knows. By the way, the very first witness to be cross-examined at the trial was one of the jewelry-suppliers. There was jewelry in the house to the value of £1382, 12 shillings—which, if bought in the shops, would have cost at least twice as much. One would need to be an owner of quite extraordinary sanguineness not to be nervous under such circumstances. (Interestingly, I think the very first thing M'Clure, the Defence lawyer, says during the trial, is to ask this witness, "Have you not made a mistake?" The witness who had talked of a brooch "with a double row of diamonds" conceded that he had indeed erred. Miss Gilchrist's brooch had a single row of diamonds. Slater's had three rows. Nerves, I suppose. But odd all the same.))

Thirty-Four

The figure of the mysterious old lady is a little broadened out by the contemporary reports, even though the newspapers, hacking around desperately for information, have obviously found few people capable of enlightening them.

(i) "She appears to have lived a somewhat lonely life, and her immediate relatives could say very little about her." (Perhaps some of her immediate relatives had rather a lot on their minds just then. (But the newspapers, interestingly, seem to have rushed onto the scene so quickly that the family had not had time to collaborate in fabricating or patching up some agreed version of events which might hide the extent of Miss Gilchrist's alienation from her kith and kin, and vice-versa.)) Truly, had she died a year before, her death would have been almost unnoticeable. Even were it something so dramatic as a dizzy spell, a fall, and a head cracking against the heavy lid of a coal scuttle.

(ii) ". . . a deep interest in religious and philanthropic work, her benevolence being well known among the poor. . ." This seems to be something more than mere pious noise offered to the worthy deceased (unlike a reference elsewhere to the effect that she was "well-known in social circles in the city", though that may only be another way of saying the same thing), for, to my recollection, at least two hospitals benefitted from the terms of her will.

(iii) ". . . owned considerable property in the East End, with which at one time she was connected." To wit, 240 Gallowgate; 60 and 68 Abercrombie Street; and 14 Margaret Street. I do not know if these were owned by her father before her, and bequeathed to her (which I rather suppose), or whether this was a venture which she embarked on for herself. However, it does suggest that if she was, as persistent rumour had it, leading a life of crime, it was not because she was otherwise without financial resource. Perhaps some of the vague "business gentlemen" who every so often visited her were those whom she employed to look after her rents, pass on the tenants' excuses, etcetera (rather as Mr. Cameron—another Cameron—does for my own landlady). One does rather wonder if one of them might not be easily mistaken for A.B. in a dim light, but there is nothing that I can do about that now.

It seems to me that, though she no doubt had many nodding acquaintances, the only friends in the whole world that Miss Gilchrist had were her ex-servant Mrs Ferguson (35 years younger than her-self), and the latter's two daughters, Marion Gilchrist Ferguson, and Maggie Ferguson. (A son had died.) Unfortunately, perhaps, for Miss Gilchrist's wishes of companionship, they lived in another town—Kilmarnock. They did, however, all go on holiday together, and it was Miss Gilchrist's intention to adopt Marion Gilchrist Ferguson. This was, presumably, an attempt to, as it were, institutionalize their friendship. The distance between the two families may have meant that Miss Gilchrist really had no-one to confide in on a day to day basis, despite having three sisters and four nephews (including A.B.)—all of them, I think, living in Glasgow—but, as far as we know, Miss Gilchrist never gave away any of her secrets to the Fergusons. (Mr. Ferguson was presumably only a man of 50 or so. I doubt if we can even add him to the most exhaustive list of very long outsiders.)

But what was Miss Gilchrist afraid of? None of the Fergusons were called at the trial, but the maid was who had worked in 49 West Princes Street before Lambie's arrival there three years previously. (I suppose Lambie answered an ad in the paper (the Glasgow Evening News, perhaps? (This was the newspaper, the December the 21st version of which Miss Gilchrist expected to be soon reading, but did not; and in the December the 22nd version of which her own death was luridly discussed.) If so, it might be worth looking through the bound volumes of mid-1905, although I am so lazy that I'm sure I won't do it myself.)) This other maid, whose name was Jane Duff or Walker (Duff was her maiden name, Walker her married one) did testify, and from her we learned that Miss Gilchrist had special jewels for special occasions, and that "she was never afraid of anyone doing any personal injury to her, but she had a great fear of the house being broken into."

We can take the latter half of that for granted—for there can rarely have been anyone in such circumstances who was *not* in great fear of being burgled. No: the interesting part of the sentence is the first part: "she was never afraid of anyone doing any personal injury to her." This is pretty unequivocal, and it comes from someone who could be reasonably supposed to know what she was talking about. "Never".

It would seem, then, that of late Miss Gilchrist's attitude had undergone something of a change, and she had lost her former composure. We recall here Lambie's visit to her own previous employer a week before the crime, (when she said "that there were strange goings-on in the house [and] that Miss Gilchrist said she was going to be murdered". It is difficult not to see this as implying at the very least the existence of an earlier, explicitly stated threat.) We may also note, for the first time, the magisterial remark in a contemporary newspaper account that, "it is inferred that she had had some information or other that she might be visited by someone who was interested in her affairs and whose designs she had reason to fear." This is such a spectacularly acute summing-up of the situation that it seems appropriate to draw another, thoughtful line across the page here, perhaps after having glancingly noted that the room in which Miss Gilchrist was murdered in 1908 had not curtains, but venetian blinds instead. I have never, to my recollection, lived in a room which had blinds, and I thus still think of them as being somehow new-fangled and modern.

Thirty-Five

One point which we are already paddling about in the shadows of is, how often, and in what circumstances, had Adams been up at Miss Gilchrist's house, prior to the night of the murder. The first account I read which mentioned this, spoke of his having visited there only 7 or 8 times in the 28 years in which Miss Gilchrist had been in occupation above. In fact, nothing I have since read has utterly contraverted this, but the thoroughgoing rarity of visit suggested by these numbers is difficult to square with some other remarks, chiefly made in the contemporary newspapers. (Of course, it is a normal facet of city life that one can live for decades the thickness of a wall away from permanently inhabited rooms that one never visits. One wonders, for instance, how often, in the 28 years of her occupation, Miss Gilchrist had ventured up the further stairway beyond her own door, and/or into the domicile above. (This, if the house next door is anything to go by, was of a quite different layout to her own, with its own internal stairway leading to several upper rooms.) It would not be surprising if she had never been there at all, or for some such forlorn total as three occasions. (Or 175 times. That is, as far as I know, rather unlikely, but not impossible.)

(I do not know the history of Adams' homes, nor have I particularly investigated it. (M.L. told me he had lived on in 51 West Princes Street until his death in, I think, 1942 (which would be six years before Slater's own death)), but the impression I took, unthinkingly, was that Adams had been in his West Princes Street house before Miss Gilchrist arrived in hers. (A braver man than I would at this point contemplate a situation in which Adams had acquired the Gilchrist flat, and Gilchrist the one on the ground floor (which, though now a state of affairs so irremediably impossible, was once presumably only a shuffle of cards away from being the situation) and what difference, if any, that would make to the case.))

The relevant remarks, however, I shall proceed to at once. Thus Adams on, I think, the night of the murder:

"On several occasions, I have had to enter her house, look under her bed, and reassure her that no-one was in hiding." (She can hardly have been in her bed, I suppose. (Come to think of it, where did Lambie sleep? In the kitchen recess? (As I understand it, the old lady slept in the front room, but kept the letter-case etc. in a spare bed-room next door, where usually no-one slept (did anyone ever?), and

113

which she used as a sort of dressing-room. Is this right?))). But what of this:

"It is known that for some months Miss Gilchrist had been in daily terror of some unwelcome visitor. She had enjoined her servant at all times to be sure the doors were properly secured, and she had on frequent occasion had the house searched before retiring at night, to make sure that no intruders were concealed anywhere." (Glasgow Evening News.) Notice the "for some months". Since when exactly? (Since she had started talking of altering her will? (Pure speculation.)) Were all Adams's visits matters of a few months in 1908? When exactly was this "three knocks" arrangement agreed on? (Presumably it had never been used prior to the night of her death. And perhaps not even then?—It is all a little *theoretical*.)) I suspect, for what it is worth, that a traditional nervousness was subsequently amalgamated with a later, more precise cause of concern.

"For several years at her own request he had repeatedly visited the house and searched every apartment to assure her no intruder was present." This talks almost as if the search were something like a nightly ritual, but it could actually, by being forced ever so little, mean much the same as what I have outlined above, perhaps coloured a little by on-the-spot over-enthusiasm on the journalist's part. Which last seems also to be somewhat the case in this:

"For, on several occasions, when more than usually startled by her loneliness, Miss Gilchrist had come down to them for refuge." (This sentence, by the way, is the only instance of phrasing in all the newspaper reports I have read, which made me realise that another human mind had chosen the words involved.) This raises an image of Miss Gilchrist sheltering timorously in the Adams house from the creaking of nocturnal boards upstairs. Presumably what is behind it is the fact that Miss Gilchrist must have come downstairs to fetch Adams up to her house, to seek out possible intruders. (One wonders how Adams felt about this. (Dark, lonely nights. Cold, murky stairway. All sorts of unwanted, suspicious noises.) One feels that the short-sighted flautist must at times have climbed those stairs, presumably followed closely by the old lady, with a feeling a good way short of eagerness.) This would suggest that Miss Gilchrist did not summon Adams by knocking on the floor. That would, after all, be a rather peremptory way to treat a neighbour. (Yet who is to be sure she was not a peremptory old woman? Something like that may even have caused her death, I suppose.)

No, the three knocks definitely seem to show the realization that there might be an occasion or occasions when help is needed immediately, without much scope being available for social niceties. This does not suggest to me so much a sudden intensifying of the fear of burglary (largely the result of a normal fear of the dark anyway), but rather the awareness that fraught situations requiring immediate outside intervention are now a distinct likelihood. In short, someone was deliberately shaking the old lady up, and she wanted to have help available lest he threaten to go too far.

Of course, the question remains—why let him in in the first place? (I presume that is what it comes down to. If Lambie is implicated, or there is an extra set of keys somewhere, I would rather not hear about it just at the moment. My nerves are bad tonight.) Or are there two men involved? If so, why let both of them in? Or, if only one of them gets in, then, (a) could the second also have got in if he had wanted to, (b) assuming he couldn't have, why then was he there, and (c), assuming he could have, why didn't he?

It comes perilously close to a mere exercise in plotting technique to provide answers to these questions. So, let us ask other questions instead. We know from Lambie (if we know anything from Lambie) that A.B. was a visitor to the house. A.B. was a nephew of Miss Gilchrist. Why was a nephew of Miss Gilchrist visiting an old lady whose relatives were not on speaking terms with her? I cannot improve on my earlier, possibly totally erroneous, suggestion vis-a-vis Miss Gilchrist's will, so we may as well ask, who would be most likely to accompany A.B. on some such visit? Well, we don't know, but who more likely than another interested member of the family, equally concerned in the success or otherwise of the venture?

Heaping speculation on speculation, we may suppose that Miss Gilchrist as a Christian woman, given to good works, could not in conscience refuse to respond to the overtures of those members of her family—particularly of the newer generations—who were now willing to talk to her. However, if these overtures had assumed menacing overtones, she might, although feeling herself unable (or somehow simply being unable) to refuse to see them at all, have drawn the line at seeing two of the aggressive young males at the same time—or of seeing any one of them for more than those brief few minutes during the absence of a servant-girl, whose departure provided them with the necessary privacy, and whose expected return provided her with the security of knowing that she would not be left alone, unguarded, for long. (Well, yes, but. (I suppose the first, who went in, had none too precise an idea as to the plan of operation likeliest to achieve the desired end (and few courses of action are more difficult for others to fathom in retrospect than the accidental), and the second was just going along for the ride, or to learn the outcome of the conversation as soon as possible. Or perhaps, to coin a phrase, they were just in it together.)

Lambie had heard an argument between Miss Gilchrist and one

of her guests previously, and had been sharply dealt with, according to her own account of matters, for curiosity about A.B. (Also, Miss Gilchrist sometimes let in her visitors by herself. (This was perhaps more from the sheer desire to protect herself from Lambie's inquisitiveness than from the need to hide a guilty secret.)) In other words, though not particularly wishing to be alone with her guests, Miss Gilchrist might well prefer to have Lambie out of earshot during private family disputes. Presumably it was thought security enough merely to have Lambie in the vicinity, with the primed Adams available as an additional potential safeguard directly beneath. (I trust Adams kept regular hours, or Miss Gilchrist knew what hours he kept.)

But, for all this, it is not clear why Miss Gilchrist would let back into the house someone who had already threatened or badly frightened her. Even if this someone was perhaps a messenger between her and others. After all, messages can be sent by other means. (Aha! "Letters scattered about" etc.) Perhaps the two men were working in tandem, and prolonging their acceptability by somehow sharing out the threats between them. (Somewhat over-subtle. Perhaps the Watcher had done the earlier threatening and was now not allowed back—a more reasonable (as she thought) emissary now taking his place, while he hovered nearby, lest his advice be needed, or forgiveness be at hand, or whatever.) After all, at least Miss Gilchrist was once again in touch with her family. (Maybe.) And, of course, for all their threats, one of them was hardly going to actually *kill* her, was he?

Thirty-Six

A couple of weeks ago, I read in that day's newspaper that an old lady of, I think, 83 had been battered to death at her home in I forget exactly which street (St. Mungo's Street, perhaps? (No: that is too far north—somewhere about John Knox Street, I think it was.)) The circumstances were familiar enough to give me a striking sense of deja vu, but, as far as I remember (and I have already forgotten almost everything I read about it) there were clear signs of a break-in. I do not recall any more of the case—truly, it could for all I know be solved by now. (Although not, I hope, as the Slater case was solved.)

I would imagine the incident took place almost exactly equidistant (5 or 10 minutes away from each) between the school where I was theoretically educated between the ages of 11 and 14 (in Duke Street—the architect being John Burnet, Sr., who designed among other things the gothic Glasgow Stock Exchange) and the Necropolis, the best-known cemetery in Glasgow—and, more specifically, that spot within it were Marion Gilchrist lies buried. Not that either old lady knew that, I don't suppose. (I wonder if the second old lady was already there when I was a schoolboy. It would be asking a long stay, but no longer than Miss Gilchrist's. For all I know, I passed her as a schoolboy. (Actually, for all I know, I passed her four or five weeks ago, when I was last in the area.)

I suspect it would be about the end of that period of my education when our house was visited by the detectives. They were, I think, investigating a murder (no less) in the St. George's Road (which thoroughfare at that time still possesseed two full sides), and were calling at every house in the neighbourhood to find what their industry might glean. Only my elder sister and myself seem to have been at home. I was beside a table in what we called "the big room"—the one behind the two windows furthest to the west of the facade (nearest Miss Gilchrist's house, as it happens—I wonder what was going on in there at those moments (it had not yet, I don't think, passed out of private possession (but I could be wrong about that)))— when my sister led the pair of them in. I was at that age when it is impossible (or, perhaps, even more impossible) to deal with any strangers, far less detectives investigating a serious crime, and I'm afraid my entrancing innate hauteur or shyness combined to exquisite effect with my adolescent gaucheness to produce a character

117

which, from the public relations point of view, fell a long way short of being a success. I spent much time smiling distantly in a manner apparently received as contemptuous, and at one point—to my complete surprise (for I think I thought I was in fact reacting with rare maturity)—I was sharply informed by one of the investigators: "This isn't a joke, you know", or words pretty nearly to that effect. I replied "I know it isn't" by pure reflex, stunned by the (to me) utterly uncalled-for tone of the intervention. Anyway, eventually the two stood up, put away their notebooks, and left, having established that we knew nothing whatever about the incident. My sister showed them out, then compounded my amazement by hurrying back into the room and rushing up to me, saying, "I hate you". I forget the discussion which followed, but I clearly remember her saying, "I hate you". (I cannot help thinking that two trained detectives should have some sort of understanding of how adolescents behave. Nor can I really think that I was posing them some unprecendented problem of comprehension. However. . .)

Which reminds me that once (only once to my recollection) we had a break-in at our house. I remember little about it—it was years before the visit of the two detectives. We were, I think, all arriving back from somewhere, perhaps a trip to the coast, and we found that something was wrong with the door. It wouldn't open more than a crack. It was snibbed by the door-chain on the inside. We, the children, were taken to the house of friends who also lived in West Princes Street, between Ashley Street (West Cumberland Street as was) and West End Park Street (the southern continuation of Rupert Street, down which the two men seen by Agnes Brown ran.) We were, if anything, elated by the novel experience, and were somewhat surprised that our parents took the adventure in such bad part. I recall another incident which occurred in one of the rooms in that house we were taken to, but I cannot remember if it happened at exactly that time, so I shall not wander even further from the point to discuss it.

But I do have another memory of the room in our own house where we were interviewed by the detectives, on another occasion when our parents happened to be absent, and we had to seek help from a neighbour. (Our parents were not absent very often, despite these two instances. Perhaps it is that very exceptionality which has made them stick so deep in the memory.) We were opening the window above the street, the left one of the pair seen from the inside. I don't know why we were opening it, but we were obviously trying to get it as high up the frame as it would go.

We never doubted that it was a simple matter, and that the frame would effortlessly slide up as far as we could push it. However, we ran into considerable resistance from it in the process, and once, when we gave it a particularly enthusiastic heave—to our horror (and horror is indeed the appropriate word), the frame detached itself completely from the woodwork at one side, and it swung into the room towards us.

It did not swing very far, for it was extremely heavy. But it swung far enough for us to be now left holding on to a very weighty square indeed of wood and glass, with no idea whatever of how to return the situation to normal—and all the while feeling an eerily excessive amount of air buffeting towards us through the empty space, the void which had been suddenly opened up in the wall of our building. It was not one of the magical moments of childhood.

I did not have a single constructive thought in my head, but my sister suggested she might go to our neighbour's door on the landing outside and try to get help from there. I, of course, agreed to this, and off she went to search for him, leaving me alone to hold the massive window. It was a long wait. (The manuscript here, by the way, reads "a long weight".) Either the window would fall in on top of me—it certainly did not seem stable—or it would fall outwards onto the street, perhaps annihilating an innocent passer-by, or carrying my youthful self with it, or both. ("Tragic Death of Young Boy"—a very plausible newspaper heading of the late 1950'—of no interest to anyone, not even the researchers who flick past it. Ah well: I myself have flicked past hundreds of such headings—and I am certainly not a diligent researcher.)

The neighbour, whose name I have utterly forgotten, duly arrived, strode resolutely up to where I was standing, and relieved me of my murderous load, easily returning it to whatever it had detached itself from. So our neighbour, at least, was of great use to us. I remember nothing of what we said, or what he said. We were, of course, more careful of windows in future.

Thirty-Seven

Of Slater, it does seem to be true that, on the first of his three (pre-trial) visits to Glasgow, in 1901, he married a native of the city. This he soon discovered to have been a grave mistake. (Apparently the real Mrs. Slater was an alcoholic, or something closely related thereto.) Strangely enough, this woman, who was apparently such a great nuisance to him, bombarding him with requests for money whenever she discovered his address (much, I learn, as my maternal great grandmother—my *mormormor*—used to behave towards my maternal grandmother (this, for a long while, was our family secret)), seems to have disappeared totally. She did not appear at or even near the trial. I have never read of anyone connected with the case so much as finding out her whereabouts, far less actually *talking* to her.

I suppose she cannot have lived in Glasgow, or Slater would never have returned here. (And, if so, she would hardly have been so completely out of the case.) But this sad experience makes it all the stranger that Slater should ever have returned there in the first place. Could he have thought, it was the last place on earth where she was likely to look for him? Was she in fact closing in on him when he left Glasgow? A peculiar subset of problems, all in all. (Yet, after his release, Slater married again, so presumably she had at least broken the surface in some shape or form before then, even if only as a death certificate.)

(And then, staying with Slater himself for a moment—to be on trial for one's life in a language which one still has difficulty with. The whole thing must have seemed like some sort of surrealist night-mare. I remember a phrase in a letter to Cameron, Slater's "only Glaswegian friend" apparently, whose hearsay indiscretions did more than anything to sink him (evidently he left Edinburgh for Glasgow immediately after the trial, not even returning to his hotel to pay his bill—an oversight which some have attributed to sheer surprise at the verdict (did defence witnesses used to have to pay their own, legally incurred expenses?)), which runs "I stand on your dear C.". This is, presumably, a literal translation of some sort of German idiom trapped in Slater's head. (Have I already mentioned before that, in addition to a detective called Cameron, my landlady's agent—the only person I have ever met who himself had met Slater—is also called Cameron? (But it's a very common name, all the same.)))

120

Thirty-Eight

Actually, only now do I realise, following a close perusal of the photographs in the library book, that my mental picture of the old lady's house was slightly wrong. The main door in the hallway is heavily biased towards the kitchen/room-containing-the-body side of the house, and away from the lobby leading to the bedroom-side. The intruder must therefore have walked some eight or ten steps to reach the outside door. (According to press reports, he kept markedly close to the wall while doing so.) Hitherto, I have always thought of it as involving only a quick couple of strides to freedom (or the possibility, sensationally realised (as it happened), of freedom). I had underestimated the sheer number of steps which the intruder must have taken during the few minutes that he was in the house.

(Also, I wonder what the result would have been if A.B. (let us call him that) had waited until Lambie had completely disappeared into the kitchen. It seems quite likely to me that that was a real possibility, physically if not psychologically. Presumably, in that case everything would have flowed along as smoothly as before. Lambie would still have mentioned a brooch; M'Lean another; and Slater would have been picked up, and possibly also identified by Lambie, who, it would transpire, was never actually right inside the kitchen after all.)

It is also worth speculating, I think, on exactly what the situation would be even if the Detective Department had been convinced of A.B.'s guilt, perhaps from remarks made to them by Lambie, if she had indeed gone into the kitchen and seen nothing of the departing guest. If no-one had reliably witnessed his flight, and if he insisted that he had been sitting quietly at home for the duration, truly, what could the police then do? There must be many cases where the police have strong prima facie suspicion against someone, but nothing more. Hence, of course, the tendency to plant evidence. The laws of admissable evidence are, alas, not found in Nature, and the fact that some cases are founded on clues which lie on one side of the law's divide, and others on the other, is certainly something which must be difficult to bear.

Indeed, even if Lambie's evidence about A.B. had been heard and believed by the police; would the evidence then have been *sufficient* to ensure a conviction for murder? Even with Watcher witnesses and a skeleton or two falling out of the cupboard, it seems to me that, particularly in the hands of a barrister with a flair for the impassioned address, the whole thing actually has the makings of a classic Not Proven case, a la Smith. (Of course, fingerprint evidence might well clinch it, but that is another question.)

Thirty-Nine

I had repaired to the library to investigate the relevant Appendix (No. 6) in the final account of the trial, which dealt with the 1914 Enquiry, with a view to investigating the asterisks. The sage investigator, deeming certain parts of the evidence unfit for public ears, replaced them with asterisks. Unfortunately, in the Appendix, I find that three modest dots replace the original asterisks, and these are not always so easy to locate among the small type. However, I will investigate them as best I can. I trust that none of them are, as it were, genuine rows of dots.

Firstly, there is Trench, visiting Nellie Lambie, along with Detective Keith—Lambie now living at the house of an aunt. This is on January the third 1909, nearly two weeks after the murder. It was the first time that Trench had spoken to Lambie:

"I touched on A.B., asking her if she really thought he was the man she saw. Her answer was: "It's gey [=very] funny if it wasn't him I saw. (Asterisks.)" (Lambie testifies later that: "The whole of that story is absolutely false", the asterisks returning in her explicit denial. Keith also denies that the suggestion was made, or the above answer given, the same asterisks returning.)

There is not much we can do here. Presumably her remark gave a reason why it would have been gey funny for the visitor not to be A.B., possibly in terms which would have allowed others to infer the noble visitor's identity. It is unfortunate that this item was suppressed, the more so in that the actual words attributed to Lambie are of some importance in determining the likelihood of the truth or falsity of the allegation. (I find it difficult to believe that, if this sentence had tended to undermine Trench's position in any way, it would have been suppressed. But alas—Millar has messed up all that; what can we do?)

"I [Miss Birrell] replied, "My God, Nellie, this is awful. Who was it, do you know him?" Nellie replied, "Oh, Miss Birrell, I think it was A.B. I am sure it was A.B." I said to her, "My God, Nellie, don't say that *** Unless you are very sure of it, Nellie, don't say that." She again repeated to me that she was sure it was A.B. The same evening Detectives Pyper and Dornan visited me, and I learned from them that she had told them it was A.B. I told a number of my friends about it, including a member of Glasgow Corporation, who communicated with Chief Superintendent Orr." (Later version: "All that is contained in it [the above report] is absolutely false.")

Again, what can we do here? If this is invention, it is brilliantly done, and it certainly succeeds in hoodwinking me . All we can do is suppose that it would bring the identity of A.B. too far out into the open for informed observers not to deduce who he must be. (Though they might well know already anyway. I wonder when the actual name (Dr. Frank Charteris) first drifted out into the light?) These suppressions seem to me most consistent with the view that Mr Millar thought Trench was lying, and wished to minimise the potential damage caused by his outrageous slanders. ("I should further say," he writes in the letter which introduces his report, "that Miss Birrell, Mrs. Gillon [Lambie, now married], and certain of the police witnesses exhibited signs of great surprise when Lieutenant Trench's statements were read to them." Pretty damn conclusive, eh? (I repeat: is it not odd that so many people had absolutely no inkling of what Lieutenant Trench was going to say? (Notice that he, (according to Alexander Cameron (another one, apparently), Chief Detective Inspector, Central Division, Glasgow Police Force, speaking at the same enquiry) had mentioned the Lambie/A.B. connection to him at the time. ("I did not speak of this story to any other officer than Trench, or to any superior officer" he adds, apparently taking care to clear his superiors twice over, (which reticence was a rare instance of self-denial in a city so full of the affair. (I trust he was one of the policemen who failed to show signs of surprise?))))

I now note, earlier in Miss Birrell's original statement: "Miss Gilchrist was not on good terms with her relations. Few, if any, visited her. (Asterisks.) I can never forget the night of the murder."

"Few, if any" is an interesting phrase. It suggests that maybe no-one did, maybe one of them did, or two, but that, really, it all comes to the same thing, doesn't it? But who rose above the familial ostracism of Miss Gilchrist (or vice versa), and why? Did the excised passage deal with this point? And how extensive was it, for the jump cut to the next line is very obvious. "Few, if any visited her, except A.B."? "Few, if any, visited her, except A.B.'s brother"? (It occurs to me that, as this document was produced by Trench, an unexpurgated version of it might well still exist somewhere.)

Just as I was about to comment on how curious it is that, in forty pages of tiny text, the only excisions should be a handful all referring to one person, I discovered the new evidence of Miss Birrell (Margaret Dawson Birrell—now at 6 Rupert Street (slightly nearer the murder site (I was once at a party on one side of the street—and once tried, unsuccessfully, to rent a room on the other (it is the street, of course, which the two men ran down, according to Agnes Brown)))) who says: "I was not called as a witness at the trial of

124

Oscar Slater. At the time of Miss Gilchrist's death I resided at 19 Blythswood Drive, Glasgow. I was in the habit of visiting Miss Gilchrist very seldom. She was not on friendly terms with her relations, on account of an estrangement as to money affairs. I visited her the Saturday previous to her death. She was 83 years of age and quite intelligent, and quite able to look after her affairs. She was active and able to go about by herself. At my visit on Saturday she was praising Helen Lambie for keeping the house clean and tidy. She never remarked about Helen Lambie's visitors, except that she once remarked about Helen Lambie having a sweetheart, a collier. As far as she said anything to me, she seemed perfectly satisfied with Helen Lambie. (Asterisks.) On the night of the murder, after seven o'clock, Helen Lambie came to my door and rang the bell violently. The maid opened the door, and Nellie Lambie rushed in and screamed out that something dreadful had happened to Miss Gilchrist. [Recap of evidence at trial follows.]"

I find that these remarks are not without their fascination. Let us begin with, "I was in the habit of visiting Miss Gilchrist very seldom." This notion of a negative habit is an unusual one. A more natural phrasing would be, "I was not in the habit of visiting Miss Gilchrist very often." Miss Birrell is trying, through verbal adroitness, to elevate her endemic absence into the habitual possibility of presence.

Nonetheless, it just so happened that one of her habitual, very seldom visits took place on the Saturday previous to her death—that is to say, two days before it. Mere coincidence, perhaps. After all, there are plenty of those in the case already. But is it not a little curious that, at the time of the trial, or in the newspaper accounts immediately after the murder, when much was made of a lonely and terrified old lady, cut off from her relatives, who knew so little about her that they were useless as sources of information and were not called as witnesses, no mention at all was made of this visit, which would, at the very least, have been most informative in establishing what the old lady's mental complexion was just before her demise? ("Former servants seem to have been almost her only visitors to her house," remarked the Lord Advocate, perhaps squeezing the truth, as usual. But Lambie at the trial, questioned as to visitors, neglects to mention that, a mere two days before the murder, one of the victim's relatives had paid her a rare visit. No—it is just: "Miss Gilchrist had not many visitors. There were some business gentlemen who came to the house. The most frequent visitor was Mrs. Ferguson, an old servant.")

Even more curious is the fact that, according to Miss Birrell's account of this final visit, Miss Gilchrist seems to have talked about little but Helen Lambie, who is awarded glowing testimonials, for no particularly obvious reason. (I suppose the "collier" mentioned as her sweetheart is the miner, Gillon, whom she later married.) The whole tenor of these remarks by Miss Birrell is to present Lambie in a good light. Did Miss Gilchrist meet her nieces once every five years or so (or eight months, or hundred and fifty-three weeks, or decade, or whatever) chiefly to praise her servant-girls to them?

(At this point, I decided I had done enough for the day (I am writing it up on the following morning) and I went over to the shelves to replace my reference books. As I was in the act of so doing, a young Indian woman leaped out towards me from behind a filing-cabinet, uttering cries of passion, and (Asterisks). As I was doing so, I noticed, at one of the three tables which are squeezed in between the bookcases and the partition-wall, M.L., my journalist informant, with whom I renewed my discussion on the case, flattered by the deft way in which he closed his notebook as we began to talk.

For hors d'oeuvre, I pointed out to him that, in the report of the 1914 Enquiry, the address of Mary Barrowman, and that of the witness Mary Couper (sic) or Dunn, is the same—19 Windsor Street. Was this, in fact, the case? If it was, it is a salutary reminder of the possible veracity of that which might at first seem outrageous coincidence. If it was not, it lessens even further one's opinion of the accuracy and trustworthiness of the magnum opus of James Millar. (Not to be confused, one trusts, with James Millar, the architect, whose new Royal Infirmary would, by April 1914, have, I suppose, been largely built. Miss Gilchrist was one of the last few thousand corpses to be taken to its now much-lamented predecessor, by Robert Adam, demolished in 1912. (I have never yet seen a kind word in print about Millar's infirmary, but I must say I think it is, from an architectural point of view, a remarkable building.)) I must check the City Directories, to find out who is listed as inhabiting 19 Windsor Street (wherever that is or was) in 1914.

(Managing to locate my Street Atlas of Glasgow, I discover that there are *two* Windsor Streets nowadays. (Two witnesses, each living at a *different* 19 Windsor Street—now that would be a coincidence indeed!) The obvious candidate is only a block away from Barrowman's old residence in Seamore Street. I know the place well, or what's left of it, but its name hadn't stuck. The other Windsor Street is a tiny thoroughfare far out in the east of the city, beside Sandymount Cemetery, which is the near inaccessible resting-place of perhaps the greatest of all Scottish painters, John Quinton Pringle. (Actually, I was in the process of writing something about Pringle when I last saw M.L., a few weeks ago.))

Anyway, M.L. saw no reason to doubt that Miss Birrell in fact visited Miss Gilchrist as she said she did, on the Saturday before the murder. Furthermore, he gently animadverted on the danger of seeing conspiracies everywhere. After all, why *should* Miss Birrell lie about this? Well, it may all just be overheated imagination on my part, I suppose, but the whole thing still *feels* wrong to me. Why should it surface only now, and only to tend to ameliorate the character of Lambie?

I did suggest, in my defence, that the whole 1914 Enquiry was an obvious conspiracy to pervert the course of justice anyway, and thus nothing should be allowed to go unexamined. From the tone of M.L.'s reply, it seemed likely to me that there was more to this affair than met the eye, or, more accurately, than met *my* eye. M.L., it transpires, is in fact collaborating on a book solely about the Slater case, for which he is in effect acting as a researcher for an author living in London. I had misunderstood earlier remarks of his about this, believing he was merely helping someone write the Slater Chapter of a book about William Roughead. It seems, alas, very likely that there are many wide and important areas to do with the Slater case that I simply know nothing about. But what can I do but stumble ahead, speculating extravagantly on the limited material available to me?

Forty

I was rather unguarded in the way I shared with a literary rival my thoughts in the matter, but it perhaps serves to repay in part certain of his hints in the past, and it is useful to have to defend your views coherently before someone not likely to let much pass him by.

In particular, I outlined the theory that possibly Adams arrived *before* the murderous assault with the chair, and perhaps precipitated the murderer into panic. I thought about this on the way home, seeking to make improvements in a largely theoretical construct. We have someone visiting the old lady to shake her out of her ridiculous intention to leave so much money to an ex-servant and her children. During a heated altercation, she stumbles, falls, and hits her head on the coal-scuttle. The intruder (who perhaps has not even touched her yet (and, even if he has, has left no visible sign of this on her body)) realises that he is not yet in trouble, for 83 year-old ladies are known to have a tendency to stumble and fall. Unfortunately (he recalls in alarm) there is possibly still in existence a letter of some sort indicating that he will be there at that time in the evening. (No: this is poor. Why could he not simply say he had not called? Or, thinking quickly, he need only realise that all it requires is for him to go out and come back half an hour later, ostensibly late for his appointment. (But that too would leave him rather open to comment. (Perhaps all this requires just far too much aplomb on his part.)))

So, is he still standing in the dining-room, sizing up the situation, when Adams rings the doorbell? Wherever he is, that ring must have been a hellish shock to him. (Perhaps even more of a shock than was the murder of the old lady. (Note that it cannot be Lambie, for Lambie has keys. And nobody visits the old lady. And nobody lives upstairs. And, though there is a family living downstairs, what have they got to do with the secretive Miss Gilchrist? (Also, one should remember the fact that, to anyone familiar with No. 49, Miss Gilchrist's house, there appears to be no-one on the ground floor—for no-one's doorway is there. There is only Miss Gilchrist's on the first floor, and the empty flat above. In other words, it feels as if there is no-one else there but Marion Gilchrist. One could easily overlook the fact that there are people directly beneath, for how could they have got there?)

No: remembering the matches, we put him in the spare bedroom already. (Adams heard no footsteps and saw no distant moving

128

shadows.) He has carefully lit the gas for illumination, leaving the box and spent match on the table beneath them, in a gesture which I shall have to interpret as calmness, in case he should need them again, or to keep before him the necessity of turning the gas off before he pockets the matches and departs. He hears the ringing at the doorbell. He waits a moment, having no alternative. The case is *locked*. The key is not available. He can hardly search Miss Gilchrist for it, can he? In moments of increasing panic, he fails to open it legitimately, and starts to hit at the lock. (What with? With a brooch picked up from the table beside him? Surely not. And yet, what else could he use? A few hard cracks directed at the vulnerable lock of the casket would be all it would take. (Of course, if he did use that, he would hardly put such a maltreated, fingerprinted object back down onto the table.)) By this time, things have, in the immortal phrase, got a bit out of hand.

One of the unfortunate things about assuming panic in the man is that it provides so easy an interpretation of any baffling detail in his subsequent behaviour. Thus, the papers and letters scattered on the floor directly beneath the broken box. Perhaps the box was so obviously broken that it made no difference now, but it is difficult not to feel that an intelligent, unflappable operator would have tried to leave everything as normal as possible, broken lock or no broken lock. Did he throw them aside in haste? Drop them inadvertently? (The idea that the broken box was a clumsy bluff, to distract attention from an intended jewel-burglary (rather than the reverse, which would seem more plausible) is found in at least one topical newspaper report. I can't see this. Why bother to make a jewel burglary (or anything else for that matter) look like a theft of documents? Who specialises in stealing documents, that the police would markedly narrow down their search in looking for them? It would make no difference that I can see to any subsequent investigation.)

As soon as Adams reaches his own house, according to newspaper reports, a loud thumping noise is heard, and his sisters at once send him back up. (At the trial, it seems to be merely their general apprehensiveness that impels him to return.) On the present—probably false—reading, this is the murderer having returned to the dining-room, where the old lady lay supine. He discovers, perhaps even by hearing her voice, that she is not dead. So, at the risk of being terminally unbelieveable, the visitor, recognising the danger that his presence in the house will be attested to by the old lady (whom, we must now say, he had in fact already struck) decides to finish her off beyond hope of redemption. (Despite the fact that this might bring the neighbour back, I presume. This will certainly cause difficulties about leaving, but at this point, the intruder has only difficulties to choose between. (And how should he know it was a neighbour, and thus be liable to return? Why might it not be a chance caller, who had definitely left, deciding that no-one was at home? (And who, by the way, if things went well, might turn out to be the police's Number One suspect.)))

(If we believe the old lady merely fell and hit her head, we must ask ourselves whether it is not likelier that, under those circumstances, the relative would merely choose to remain there, and perhaps even to help her, than that he would suddenly discover a hitherto undreamt-of psychopathic side to his nature and batter her to death. Of course, we might say he doubted the possibility of others believing in his innocence, but, even so, to a normal human being it would not even occur that there was any choice but to take that risk. He may simply have felt himself to be too compromised already, by other considerations of which we alas know nothing, but I think we have to assume that, in fact, he was already physically implicated in the old lady's demise—which is to say, that he had caused her fall.)

The old lady's head was beaten in with unexampled savagery. This is an area where one must go carefully, and perhaps ought not to visit at all; but I would think that the gap between battering a defenceless old lady's face in once, or doing so a thousand times, is far less than that between doing it once and not doing it at all. If you do it even once, then it seems to me to be largely a question of chance, or a trick of circumstance, as to when you bring yourself to stop doing it. It has been argued that the extreme brutality is to be ascribed to a monstrous irrationality (actually, I think it comes closer to a monstrous rationality), perhaps even to a fit. This is possible, but it could just as well result from extreme cold-bloodedness. (Certainly, the idea that someone who bludgeons an old lady's face ten times is twice the criminal of someone who humanely restrains himself to so doing a mere five times is grotesque.) The decision is taken that the old lady *must* be silenced. Thus her head must be attacked. This chair will do as well as anything, particularly as it saves me the need of even having to kneel down—and, in fact, spares me the sight of the moment of impact. (On second thoughts, this may be as much a drawback as an advantage, for, presumably, he would have to check at some point to see what sort of effect he was producing.) A few downward thrusts, a rug thrown over the face (for such was the probable order of events) and that is that.

This reconstruction is, of course, full of errors and is probably grossly wrong. The murderer goes into the hall, (perhaps) puts on his coat, and waits, not knowing that, in fact, the old lady is *still* alive. Why is he waiting? Why not try to leave at once? (In the normal version, he is interrupted by sounds at the door while still searching

130

among the documents. This raises in a sharper form the question—did he find whatever he was looking for, and makes it rather less likely that he did. But to me it does seem likely that he was actually waiting anyway.) The possibility of meeting someone in the stair is manifest, and, anyway, we could assume he knew that Lambie (who, incidentally, if he gets away unnoticed, would be a major suspect in some form) ought to be back soon. He is unclear about how much time has passed. His best chance of escape is while the horrified Lambie is in the dining-room, coping—or, more probably, not coping—with what she has just found. (It's an interesting thought, if such an improbable one that I shall not pursue it, that the interference with the casket was a ploy to tend to incriminate Lambie.)

And the second man? Hardly a lookout, for he did nothing about Adams. (Perhaps a lookout lost in theory—an incompetent lookout. Incompetence, like chance, is difficult to make exact allowances for.) Is he either a figment of Agnes Brown's imagination, or a completely unfunctional, extra observer of the scene? I don't know. If A.B. knew he would be upstairs for only a few minutes, it is even possible that this was someone whose company he was in, and did not wish to lose merely for so short an interlude. But, if he was there, one wonders what effect the revelation as to why his friend had reappeared in such haste subsequently had on their relationship. In the wrong hands, this sort of thing could even lead to blackmail. What on earth did they talk about on their subsequent reunions (perhaps for the next fifty years)?

Forty-One

One or two other points which occurred to me in the wake of my conversation with the expert:

It might be remarked that things would have been a lot simpler for the police if Cameron had merely denied that he had discussed the subject with Trench at all. This is certainly true. Perhaps Cameron was such an honest man, something in the Trench mould, that he refused to lie about so serious a subject (perhaps he was simply a friend of Trench's) and would go no further than exonerate his superior officers from opprobrium by stating that he had never discussed the subject with him. This does tend to suppose, however, that the police had no choice but to let him be questioned, which one jibs at a little. Perhaps I am indeed missing everything of any importance. (And perhaps I could just as well repeat here my recent remark about incompetence.)

Also, I am persistently niggled at by the knowledge that he might possess police information which leads him to strongly believe that the person whom Lambie saw leaving the house could not have been A.B., alias Dr. Frank Charteris, late of St. Andrew's University. It is, of course, impossible for me to confront this difficulty head on, as I have not the least clue as to what this "information" is, and it may be devastating (or non-existent). All I can do at present is comfort myself with the perhaps specious consolation that it seems to me a clear enough implication from the behaviour of the murderer, that this man would certainly be capable of talking his way out of any difficulty that gave him scope for manoeuvre. One would be surprised if this murderer had done all he was capable of in the interests of self-preservation, when he raced down West Princes Street past the empty space where Mary Barrowman was supposed to have been standing.

(And I think I should add that an obvious way to open a fragile box would be to hit the lock against the edge of a table. But I have never seen any discussion of how the box was opened, so it would seem that here speculation can roam, freely unchecked. (By the way, I quite forgot to mention that it may well have been in the panic induced by the arrival of Adams that the murderer forgot all about the matchbox and used match.))

132

Forty-Two

I broke off the discussion of the asterisks before I had finished it. This was partly through accidental circumstance, and partly because I discovered, somewhat to my chagrin, that the elusive Superintendent Douglas actually made a statement at the 1914 Enquiry, which fact had hitherto contrived to escape my notice. But first I must deal with the relevant part of Lambie's own testimony. (I leave out the "gey funny" business, treated above.) This runs as follows:

"The statement in Appendix No. 2 to Detective Inspector Trench's precognition (that is to say, the "My God, Nellie etc." discussed earlier) being read over to Mrs. Gillon, she states that there is absolutely not one word of truth in it. (What, not even: "My [Miss Birrell's] mother was a sister of the deceased"? Nor, perhaps: "Miss Gilchrist's servant, Nellie Lambie, came to my door about 7.15"?) She never said to Miss Birrell that it was A.B., and the whole story is absolutely false. I had seen A.B. in Miss Gilchrist's house on one occasion before (Asterisks) The man I saw leaving the house was not at all like, nor did I ever see A.B. dressed like the man I saw (more asterisks) A gentleman who had apartments in Miss Birrell's house took me to my aunt's house. etc."

The tendency to read the first pre-asterisk sentence as meaning that Lambie had only ever seen A.B. once before is so strong that I for quite a while assumed that that was what it came to. Of course it is not unreasonable to do so, as this is in fact what it does say as far as it goes, yet the very next sentence, "Nor did I ever see A.B. dressed like the man I saw. . .", which we must suppose refers to sightings of A.B. only one of which was in Miss Gilchrist's house, was sufficient to raise a doubt in my mind at least. But be that as it may, this and the next sentence make it quite clear that Lambie had seen A.B. fairly often, wherever it was, and that she had absolutely no doubt as to his appearance. It therefore seems to me that, if we accept Trench's submission of what Lambie said to Miss Birrell on the night of the murder as being true, then that, taken together with these more recent conclusions, makes it next-door to certain that, if the intruder was not A.B., then it was at least somebody who looked very like him. (The only alternative to this that I can think of—apart from the notion of a straightforward malicious lie on Lambie's part to get A.B. into great trouble, which I discount as being just too gratuitous—is that Lambie might, for some undisclosed

133

reason, have automatically supposed it to be A.B., and that nothing about the intruder's appearance served to controvert the supposition. (This seems to me, I must say, to be scarcely less gratuitous than the previous suggestion.))

Of course, if the intruder was wholly unknown to Lambie, as she later claimed, her behaviour as he walked out past herself and Adams defies rational analysis, and we may as well seek the answer in the realms of the paranormal, and leave psychology and logic alone. It is also to be noted that her view at the Enquiry, officially at least, was that the intruder was in fact Oscar Slater. Now, we can certainly believe that Oscar Slater never dressed like A.B. (although Lambie was not necessarily implying that a continental mode of dress was unknown to her from her recollections of A.B., she testified to the intruder's wearing a flat cap and a grey coat, of widespread local usage, and not quite Slater's style), and to say that Oscar Slater was "not at all unlike" A.B.—which is what we must suppose her to be claiming in 1914, if we are to attribute any meaning to her words at all—is a little flamboyant, not to say downright incredible. But let us get back to our asterisks.)

As printed in Roughead's book (perhaps the original report was less ambiguous in this connection) it is not even absolutely certain that the sentence preceding the first asterisks is complete as it stands. The whole context is unsure. The sentence immediately before it in its turn talks of Lambie in reported speech: "She never said. . ." Then, suddenly, an exquisite disjunction throws unwarned in front of us Lambie in direct quotation: "I had seen. . ." (Note that the sentence between the asterisks, also given in direct speech, cannot possibly be an actual quote from Lambie, unless we are to believe that she spoke at times like a legal document—"was not at all like, nor did I ever see".)

What do the first asterisks conceal? Presumably some overexplicit reference to the only occasion on which Lambie had seen A.B. in the house before. But it could equally well be a particularization of only one such occasion which it seemed uniquely appropriate to recall. (For instance, "I had seen A.B. in Miss Gilchrist's house on one occasion before when they were having an argument etc." This is pure speculation of course, and it is most probably entirely wrong, but it does fit. And Mr Millar's reticence only tends to encourage the proliferation of such inventions to fill his gaps. Why should we take his word for anything? Why should we *have* to? However, in the end, yet again we just do not know.)

But, if the first asterisks are mysterious, what on earth are we to make of the second set? Again a blatant jump in the narrative follows, leading us to wonder just how much has been excised. It is so black a hole that even the most riotous imagination can hardly summon up anything adequate to fill it with. It is, in short, Mr. Millar's undoubted masterpiece in the genre. His technique, unsteady at first, has by now developed to such an extent that he leaves no loose ends, no untidy stragggling half-clues to spoil the effect. It will be difficult for him ever to improve on *this,* one fears.

Forty-Three

I have read over Superintendent William Miller Douglas's statement
to the 1914 Enquiry several times now, half expecting it to solve the
ultimate problem, half expecting it to disappear in a twist of smoke.
It has, however, thus far done neither. It is in fact a depressingly
ordinary statement, coming from one who had attained almost legendary status in my Slaterean pantheon, as being at the heart of the
secret. This secret, by the way, according to him did not exist—but
let us go through his statement in an orderly, if selective, manner.

It was Superintendent Douglas who "took charge of the early
enquiries into the murder of Miss Gilchrist". (Within a couple of
days at the most, Ord seems to have been running the show.) He
tells us he received information of the murder about 7.50 p.m., and
went to West Princes Street forthwith. This is presumably half an
hour after the police were first informed, which sounds fair enough.
What state, however, is the murderer in by now, as Douglas goes
past the small crowd and in through the open door? If we believe
in Brown's running couple (and I do), it would seem that they had
no other transport immediately available (and therefore, presumably, had walked to Miss Gilchrist's house). This in turn suggests
that they had not travelled too far. (For what it is worth, they seemed
in no hurry to get onto a tram-route, although that could be sheer
shunning of the light.)

Anyway, we might as well have them arrived together in a safe
haven before Douglas reaches the dead body. Now, whoever walked
out that house knew he had passed within whispering distance of a
man at the door, who, for all he knew, must have got a very good
look at him. (He can hardly have suspected that Adams was a short-
sighted gent, caught without his glasses (a twinge of suspicion reaches
me here about this, but passes at once. I believe this is indeed what
it amounted to. (Had Adams thought first to put on his glasses before
going upstairs, it is possible that the case would have been solved
within an hour.))) We may suppose, from the nature of his action,
that the killer's thoughts were bent less towards remorse for what
he had just done, than towards a plan to enable him to escape the
consequences. What if this man should subsequently identify him?
What could he do?

It takes only a moment's thought to realise that he could do nothing
but deny it outright, basing his case on the improbability of certainty

in identifying a complete stranger seen in less than glaring light for at most ten seconds. (Of course, an alibi woud not go amiss. But, even without one, on the supposition that Adams was wholly unknown to the stranger, he could reasonably, albeit not infallibly, suppose in turn that he himself was unknown to Adams. (As I have said, the houses were completely separate, and Miss Gilchrist does not appear to have been a woman who shared with her neighbours what little social life she had. (We could dot the i's by adding that if A.B. and Adams did know each other, then A.B., if it was him, would know, if he kept his wits about him, that Adams had come up without his glasses and had failed to recognise him.)

In short, if it were only the question of Adams, the murderer could sit tight, lie through his teeth, and pray nothing was discovered to link him to the case in such a way that might carry a jury. But there was also Lambie. I'm afraid I cannot see beyond the fact that Lambie and whoever walked out the house knew each other. I suppose the intention of the intruder was to leave unobserved, but that Lambie's unexpected preference for the kitchen rather than the dining-room somewhat threw out his timing. On this view, the man must have *known* that Lambie could identify him. What, if anything, could he do about that?

Well, since we have come up so high already, let us add another storey to this castle in the air. Here, merely to insist that the woman was making an honest error would not have done. She knew him personally, and, presumably, could easily prove so. The case must therefore be that she was deliberately lying. Why? Out of personal animus against him? Perhaps: but that would be rather an extreme way of exercising a personal spite. To protect someone else whom she knew it to be? This is more likely, as it makes her less of a female Iago. (This view, I think, is still a current and plausible enough one. It may, I suppose, even be true. But if so, and Trench is to be believed, then the girl was so quick off the mark with her A.B. story that she was either uniquely inspired, or else party to the plan beforehand. I do not give much credence to any of that.)

(At this point, not without considerable nervousness, I begin to sense some vague rationale behind the tendency to exonerate Lambie which is a feature of this enquiry. (So far, I have discovered Miss Birrell, Ord, Dornan, and Douglas, all doing it.) It suggests that there is an element elsewhere in the enquiry tending to incriminate her or blacken her character. But wherever this is, if it exists, I haven't found it yet. Which inexorably leads me to suspect that it might be found among the excisions. (Immediately after writing this, I realise that, of course, the very existence of the tribunal is itself a potential insult to Lambie's good name, as, if Trench's submissions are found good, she is shown to be a practised liar and a perjurer. That would in itself, I think, be sufficient to explain the interest taken by so many into her character. Perhaps I should score out this paragraph.)

(As you see, I did not do so. I turned to reread Miss Birrell's remarks about Lambie, and I must say I suspect they open the door again. They sound more like special pleading than testimony as to character. I'll need to pause and think about this one.)

We left the murderer wrestling with the problem of what to do in the light of the (probable) identification of him by Lambie. We came to the decision that he would decide he had no choice but to claim that Lambie was doing this in the attempt to shield someone else whom she had recognised. (He knows that Lambie said nothing when he walked past. (If she had as much as remarked "A.B.?" in a puzzled tone, in front of Adams, his position would be even more desperate. But she had been warned against taking too great an interest in her mistress's visitors. (Can the visitor quite have rid himself of the fear that she told Adams who it was after he had gone? (Yet, the longer the delay, the better his chances of suggesting it was a ploy. (However, note that Lambie did *not*, as it happens, mention this to Adams. This, in fact, is actually a distinct point against those theories which seek to have Lambie deliberately putting the blame on A.B. for whatever reason. Not only, if she wished to do so, would she be more likely to begin the process at once, but the very neglect of mentioning it to Adams would greatly compromise the effectiveness or credibility of then mentioning it later to anyone else. (Of course, one can come up with contrary points— such as that she was working to a pre-formed plan that she did not dare try to alter (which seems to me to require one to believe that she knew in advance that she was going to find something criminal waiting for her when she returned to the house that evening) or that she only elaborated the details during her flight to Miss Birrell's. But notice this flight which she has already started on. Is it not more like the behaviour of someone who had to tell someone what she had just seen, but dared not talk to anyone but a member of the family concerned, who, knowing the people involved and (some of) the implications of what she had seen, could better advise her what to do than could any neighbour, however well-meaning, none of whose business any of this was?))))))

Is this (purely theoretical) attempt of his a counsel of utter desperation, depending on luck for success, or has he any prior reason to believe in its plausibility? His hand is perhaps forced anyway, but it requires little additional effort to suppose that he had seen or heard enough to know that Lambie did not inhabit a world utterly unfrequented by males. Indeed, we may as well add that it might have been some such recent occurrence or remark that suggested this fantasy of mine to him in the first place. Anyway, I can do nothing better to settle his mind. An attitude of total astonishment, a solemn statement drawing attention to his utter respectability in as subtle but forceful a manner as possible, and a remark to the effect that Miss Gilchrist had in the past, as far as he knew, shown unease as to the company which Lambie kept. Then a meeting with Lambie during which he would run rings round her, and try his damnedest to get her to retract her statement (perhaps helped to a surprising extent by detectives of distinctly less than average abilities). And once she has withdrawn the statement in the presence of the police, what can happen to him? (Perhaps his position is saved even without an explicit retraction.) What other evidence is there, given the police handling of the case? A life with mild suspicion hanging permanently over him is not perfect, by any means, but it is preferable to being hanged.

Of course, what we have created here seems to fall not far short of Moriarty, master criminal: it would certainly be a relief to know that he had a brilliant legal brain (or, bearing in mind his behaviour during the murder, that he had some training in autopsy work). Perhaps he simply bemusedly protested his innocence, and the detectives, finding him so plausible and Lambie's bizarre behaviour so implausible or downright suspicious, in effect did his work for him. (One recalls the "scoffing" remark. The Enquiry report has several instances of detectives stating unequivocally that they are quite convinced that A.B. had nothing whatever to do with the murder. Now, this is all very well. But we are never given their reasons. I don't think their reasons are anywhere even hinted at. We have to take it on trust. And it occurs to one to remark that to state unequivocally, for example, that one has nothing in one's pockets is a poor second to turning one's pockets inside out to demonstrate as far as possible the truth of one's contention. And that to keep on insisting on the fact, and to keep on not turning out one's pockets is a course of action liable to be misinterpreted. If you are so certain, WHY are you so certain? Merely to insist on the certainty, and never once give a reason which clarifies it, suggests that it is at least possible that no such reason actually exists. Why should we take these men's word for it? (If A.B. could prove that he was, say, in Chojnice, Poland, on the night of the murder, does anyone doubt that that fact would have turned up somewhere—in the Enquiry report perhaps, if nowhere previous, to settle the point once and for all. He would therefore hardly *need* to be protected, for his innocence would (I presume) at once be obvious to everyone. (It seems to me more and more likely that the police simply talked Lambie out of the A.B.

story from a sense of the innate rightness of their preconceptions. (However, yet again: I don't know.)))

(Note the famous statement of Superintendent Ord made when Trench handed to him the written report of his visit to Miss Birrell on the 27th of December: "I have been ringing up Douglas, and he is convinced that A.B. had nothing to do with it". The phrasing of this is actually rather eloquent. It is a question of Douglas already being "convinced" rather than (unless Ord is being more subtle than I suspect him capable of being) his inducing Ord to share his conviction by vouchsafing some weighty proof. (Or Ord's later remark to Trench, after the latter's first meeting with Lambie. "Douglas has cleared that up, and what can we do?" Again, Douglas is, it seems, the only man allowed onto a horse. The rest must march obediently in step behind him.)

Forty-Four

As, by some miracle, we have arrived back with Superintendent Douglas, it might be as well to continue our investigation of his statement. Of "Detectives Pyper and M'Vicar and Dr. Pirie", who were in the house when he arrived, the last vanish from sight at once.

He inspects the body, then searches the house. ". . . on the dressing table in the spare bedroom, from which the man was said to have come, I found a gold bangle in case, a lady's gold watch and albertina—these were in a small glass tray—a lady's gold ring and two rings, of no value, in another dish, a work-box with the lid wrenched off, a box of Runaway [!] matches and a spent match of the same kind, a number of papers lying on the floor underneath where the work-box was." (Presumably "a lady's gold ring and two rings, of no value, in another dish" should be "a lady's gold ring, and two rings of no value, in another dish." The thief had thus spared himself the immense physical effort involved in picking up a bangle, a watch, and a ring, all made of gold. Allergic to the stuff, no doubt. ("The motive for the crime is as plain as daylight," as the Lord Advocate's closing address puts it.))

The Superintendent then ruminates on the complete absence of blood in this room, although he is debarred by the received wisdom on the case from suggesting either that more than one person was involved, or that the ransack preceded the bloody assault. We next come to this: "I saw Helen Lambie there, and she made no statement as to the man who left the house being any particular man. I saw Miss Birrell there, and she did not say that Helen Lambie made any such statement to her. Nor did the gentleman who was with Miss Birrell. I left the house in charge of uniformed constables [three dots here] Next morning I received, from Detective Pyper, a written report of a statement which had been made to him by Miss Margaret Birrell on the night of the murder."

Incidentally, it was while reading this that I first fully took on board the notion that Miss Birrell had visited the Gilchrist flat on the night of the murder. Checking a photocopy which I took yesterday of a page which graciously combines Trench's deposition and her own, immediately following, (it being Good Friday, the library is closed for a few days, and I have photocopied a couple of pages of the book, hoping thus to tide myself over the gap), I discover that she does (in 1914) in fact say she went there, taking Cowan, her lodger at the time, along with her. I am trusting to memory here, but I am quite certain that not a word of this was breathed at the trial. Indeed, Lambie's visit to Miss Birrell is itself touched on only very sparingly. (I remember clearly that I was once sure it had not been mentioned at all, which should perhaps be a lesson to me. But this visit of Miss Birrell, so wonderfully revealed to us five years after the fact, particularly when combined with her equally tardily admitted visit on the Saturday previous, makes her absence at the trial all the more unusual. (Indeed, so far as I recall, her name was not so much as mentioned.))

However, let us examine the asterisks, which, after all, was my original intention here. I'm afraid they will not detain us for long, for once again Mr. Millar, by now at the height of his powers, has done his work well. 71 years later, and still we are not to know the full facts of perhaps one of the most striking of the known miscarriages of justice (well, known to *me*, let us say) in any country within the Western tradition.

Passing on to consider more of what Mr. James G. Millar has so kindly left us, we soon read: "I am perfectly sure it is untrue to say that on the 22nd December, accompanied by Detectives Pyper and Dorman, I drove in a taxi cab to the house of A.B. and that that was done in view of information supplied by Helen Lambie." This meeting I take to be the heart of the mystery, and so I would be loth to lose it. We might note, however, that Dorman's name was actually Dornan, and so Bertrand Russell could easily show that the literal truth of this statement was not in itself inconsistent with such a meeting, with one Dornan there, actually having taken place. He would also note, if he could turn his attention aside from whatever problem he was busy with in the real world, that in the form of statement given, when divorced from its inferences, what is being denied is primarily that the three men "drove in a taxi-cab to the house of A.B." I shall cling to the possibility that they arrived there by some other means of transport—possibly by camel.

At this point we meet the second batch of asterisks. "The statement made by Lieutenant Trench with reference to this supposed visit to A.B.'s house has been read over to me and it is absolutely without foundation. . . The statement contained in No. 2 of the Inventory [i.e. "Oh my God, Nellie" etc.] annexed to Lieutenant Trench's precognition has been read over to me and I never heard of it previous to this enquiry being started." Thus all my attempts at diplomacy in the previous paragraph go for nothing. Someone is in an adversarial relationship with the truth. (One might think Trench was simply misinformed, but he clearly states, "I am aware that on the 22nd December etc." which is utterly unequivocal.)

Again, we are helpless. What has the impartial flow of justice to do with us? Nanny and Mr. Millar know best. Trench's original statement is mentioned, then there is the lacuna, then the second, supplementary statement of his inventory is referred to. This, if it suggests anything, would tend to direct us to the first supplementary document, and, as far as I recall, this is a copy of the police descriptions of men wanted for questioning, with the Lambie/Adams suspect carefully kept separate from the new, Barrowman, suspect. (Did the Superintendent perhaps suggest that this too was an invention of Trench's fevered mind? *(In fact, this is solely the pre-Barrowman suspect.))* But I find it more likely that the asterisks refer to an additional point made with regard to the sentence immediately preceding. What exactly this point was, I suspect we will now never know.

We pass by without comment a variety of "never saw it before in my life's before alighting for a moment at that resonant phrase of Lambie's, to Trench, on his first visit to her (Jan. 3rd, 1909), to wit: "It's gey funny if it wasn't him I saw." Here, uniquely, the phrase is not followed by asterisks. Alas, the next sentence, though full of interest, is obviously not the words excised everywhere else. Presumably Mr. Millar simply thought it not worth the trouble to put the whole of Lambie's supposed utterance (if that is what it amounts to) to the busy Superintendent. Or possibly he did, but forgot the asterisks in writing out the documentation. (Perhaps—vide the "Dorman" slip above—he was a little tired, after a hard day wrestling with Truth.)

"I was in charge of the inquiry at the Western District Office into the murder of Miss Gilchrist, and I can say that full inquiry was made into the movements of A.B. by the police, and I am satisfied that he had nothing whatever to do with the murder," is the aforementioned next sentence. Several writers, Roughead in particular, have gleefully seized on this, and have asked, why, if nobody mentioned A.B.'s name at the time, was it thought necessary to enquire into his movements?

The preferred riposte to this is to point out that, in a case of this nature, the police would closely investigate the movements of anyone at all connected with the dead woman, with the witnesses etc., as a matter of mere routine, hoping that something might turn up in the process to give some point to their researches. As a rejoinder, this is very strong. It is a pity he did not add some such phrase as "as a matter of course" before the second comma, but he may reasonably have felt this to be obviously implied. If A.B. was a relative of the murdered woman, living close by, he would inevitably be subjected to close scrutiny. (Before leaving this sentence, we may wish to compare its first clause ("I was in charge of the inquiry at the Western

143

District Office into the murder of Miss Gilchrist,") with the very interesting first sentence of this very deposition, which begins, "I was Superintendent of the Western District in December, 1908, and accordingly took charge of the early inquiries into the murder of Miss Gilchrist". This slight firming up of the point for safety's sake (if that is what it is) is entertaining to note, but of next to no importance. (We may also wish to remark again, what a pity it is that Superintendent Douglas does not at this point enlighten us even a little as to what it is that makes him so satisfied as to A.B.'s innocence. (There aren't even any asterisks here.)))

What are we to make, however, of the very next sentence? "Inquiry was made by the police with regard to any possible relationship between Helen Lambie and Oscar Slater, and the police were satisfied that there was no evidence that Lambie knew Slater or had been in his house, or had anything to do with him whatever, previous to the murder." This brings us back at last to the question of Lambie's character, but it does so by an extremely curious route. As far as I remember, there was nothing in Trench's submissions that so much as hinted at Oscar Slater and Helen Lambie knowing each other, or having visited each other. There is no sign that such a thought ever crossed his mind, and no reason why it should have done. Why should anyone feel called upon to deny allegations other than those that had actually been made by Trench? But Douglas is not alone in this. We thus find Superintendent Ord informing the same enquiry—it is almost the very first thing he reportedly says—that, "So far as the police know, there is no ground whatever for saying Helen Lambie knew Slater previous to the murder or had ever been in his house." I don't doubt this for a moment (which is a pleasant change where this man is concerned) but who was saying this? Was it part of the enquiry's remit to scotch ridiculously wide-of-the-mark rumour, or slap down completely irrelevant speculation?

If the desire is merely to exonerate Lambie generally as to character, to lessen the possibility that she is the perjuror which Trench's submissions would make her out to be, there is hardly any need to be so flamboyantly precise. Something along the lines of what Miss Birrell said, or Detective Dornan, would be quite sufficient for establishing character. ("With regard to Helen Lambie, I made careful enquiries into her character, both at her neighbours, young men she knew [notice this plural], and shopkeepers in the locality, and I found that although she was fond of joking she was a perfectly respectable girl." (Dornan))

No: it seems likely to me that the suggestion that Lambie already knew Slater before the murder was part of the circumstances under review. Now, assuming this, where could such a suggestion have

144

come from? I can see no sign of it in the text, so it is not unreasonable to look for it among the asterisks. (Of course, to the upper echelons of the Glasgow police, the terms Slater and murderer were synonymous, so the suggestion that Lambie already knew the murderer would to them be equivalent to the suggestion that she knew Slater. The contention that Lambie knew the murderer may already sound somewhat famliar, but even these detectives can hardly have supposed that for Lambie to deny having recognised A.B. from previous meetings necessitated her denying that she recognised Oscar Slater from previous meetings too. There is some special point being made here. (Notice the unfathomable shared insistence that she had never been in Slater's house. We have so far heard no-one ever suggest that she had, and, to the best of my knowledge, no-one ever will.)

As the rest of Douglas's remarks are not very interesting (with the exception of the penultimate sentence, "I do not remember matches similar to the box of matches left in Miss Gilchrist's house being found in Oscar Slater's house, but it has to be remembered that, since Slater left, the house had been occupied by Mrs. Freedman and her friends," with its disingenuous "I do not remember" (as if there may have been, but it had temporarily slipped his mind—had there been, we may be fairly sure the Superintendent would have remembered it), and its attempt to outflank even such a small point in Slater's favour as the matches provide, suggesting the continuing desire to find Slater guilty) and there is only one more asterisk passage that I am aware of, we may as well clean that up here.

It occurs in the immediately following statement of John Pyper, Chief Detective Inspector, Western Division of the Glasgow Police, which has already been glanced at with some interest. "I saw Helen Lambie that night, and I took a full statement from her as to what occurred from the time she left the house till she returned. She told me she did not know who the man was, and she did not think she would be able to identify him." No intervention here by Mr. Millar. And no asterisks either, bless his heart. I suspect he missed the force of this. (And yet, all it does is undermine Lambie's evidence as to identity even further. And truly, Lambie's evidence was so compromised that, even if this utterance had been mentioned at the trial, it would almost have got lost in the crowd, and the jury that could swallow the camel would hardly strain at this gnat. (Of course, there could well be an overwhelming reason why it could not be mentioned at the trial—to wit, it had not yet been thought up. But I suspect that if Lambie had never made such a remark to Pyper at some time or other, such an unfortunate revelation would never have emerged in the trial. (It strikes me that it is possible that Lambie could have gone back to the house after talking to Miss Birrell, with the decision made, from whatever pressures, not to mention what she thought she had seen. Or still uncertain whether to name A.B. to the police or not. She thus may have, perhaps from motives of loyalty, have told some of the police one thing, and others another. This would in itself tend to make the police highly sceptical of any name she gave them—perhaps she at some point decided to come clean at last by simply admitting that it was A.B.—making them suspect she was just telling yet another story (and a particularly improbable one this time, possibly in desperation), and putting them in some doubt as to the simplicity of her motives.))

Pyper's statement continues: "I examined her very severely on that occasion, and she never said anything to me about A.B. being the man. I also examined Miss Birrell, and her statement is on page 305 of the Copying Book of date 21st December, 1908. In that statement Miss Birrell says, "I" [sic] have no suspicion of any person who would have injured her." So far as these two witnesses are concerned I never heard anything then or since that would cast the slightest suspicion on A.B. I have carried on a good part of the inquiry, and from all I have heard I have not a shadow of doubt that A.B. had nothing to do with the murder. . . On 24th December I went to Mary Barrowman's employer's shop etc." I particularly regret these asterisks, for they come at precisely the moment when Pyper would give the reasons for his confidence in A.B.'s innocence, assuming he ever gave any. But, quite apart from this, there is something about the tone of this passage which reminds me with painful immediacy of M.L.'s utter certainty that the A.B. business is complete red herring, and that A.B. had nothing to do with it. (And yet. And yet. We may remember that Pyper, during the trial, insisted that as he was standing, with Lambie and Barrowman on either side of him, in the corridor outside the door through which Slater was to be led in to hear extradition proceedings in New York, both Lambie and Barrowman *simultaneously* touched him on the arm, and both, *simultaneously,* exclaimed, "That is the man!" ("It may seem strange, but I can assure you that it is the truth.") This takes some believing, and the American Detective, Pinckley, one of the men accompanying Slater, remembered quite a different version of events. In short, the possibility arises that Pyper on occasion is capable of lying with considerable aplomb. Perhaps it is part of his job.)

Forty-Five

I have been brooding overnight on the twinges of cramp in my leg, and on the possibility that Helen Lambie did not at first identify A.B. as the man she saw in the hall. I had once or twice before been vaguely struck by the fact that, according to Trench, Detectives Pyper and Dornan took a taxi to A.B.'s house on Tuesday the 22nd, which is to say, the day after the murder. If Lambie mentioned A.B.'s name to the police at 7.30 of the previous evening, is this not a trifle leisurely? (Perhaps it isn't. Perhaps, also, (though I rather doubt this) one waits to see what the suspect will do next. (However, checking through the documentation available to me, I find that, according to Trench's description of Miss Birrell's statement to him on the 23rd, Detectives Pyper and Dornan visited her on the evening of the crime, and she learned from them that Lambie had already identified A.B. As I believe Trench more or less implicitly, I must therefore revise my view somewhat.)

Notice that, in the "My God, Nellie" version, Miss Birrell clearly states that Pyper and Dornan visited her in her home. (Cowan, the lodger, nowhere appears. No earlier visit to West Princes Street is mentioned.) This may or may not be a little odd, given that, according to the evidence at the tribunal, both Miss Birrell and Pyper had been at the Glasgow flat earlier, presumably at the same time. Indeed, Pyper's testimony can only, without forcing, be taken to mean that he interviewed Miss Birrell after Lambie at West Princes Street.) If two interviews were involved (which I tend to doubt) then perhaps something like a change of story from Lambie made the second one suddenly advisable.

But this is such shadow-chasing speculation that I don't think I ought to pursue it further now. I have given much thought to this apparent need to brighten up Lambie's public image in general, and to state explicitly, in particular, that she did not know Slater and had not visited his house, but the subject continues to elude me. I will thus now turn aside for a while to read a book which I discovered in a second-hand bookshop earlier this afternoon, and which I have thus far, with tremendous self-discipline, forborne to look at. To wit: a copy of an American paperback edition of Peter Hunt's "Oscar Slater, The Great Suspect", which I shall now reread at my own leisure (I read a library copy in earlier, more innocent days), keeping Lambie's position particularly in mind, and hoping that, when I have finished it, I shall have sufficient thoughts on how to continue.

Forty-Six

Well, I have read it again by now, and it suggested a few new points, and repeated a few old points that I grasped for the first time. Some of these concerned the 1914 Secret Enquiry, but about the particular problem that has continued to worry me—why it should be thought necessary to deny that Lambie had known Slater or had been in his house previous to the murder—there is nothing, except the bare reporting that Superintendent Ord had said that the police had satisfied themsleves at the time that A.B. had nothing to do with the murder, and that Lambie had never known Slater prior to the murder. But why bother about that last? To clear her of suggestions of collusion with Slater, the supposed murderer, and of identifying someone else to protect him? (But, of course, the police position is that she did not identify someone else. And who is suggesting, or suggested, collusion with Slater, the man whom she after all so mightily helped to convict? Was this supposed collusion police suspicion at the time, perhaps to explain her strange silence? (Which, to the police, must remain strange, I suppose.) But who cares about that now? And, even if that is the case, and it might well not be, whence comes the need to deny that she had been in Slater's house? I still cannot see where that suggestion is likely to have come from.

(My investigations of the asterisks in this connection did not lead to any sudden blinding light. It is, after all, possible for instance that she said, "It's gey funny if it wasn't him I saw. I've been in his house"—or, to make it as plausible as we can, "The man I saw leaving the house was not at all like, nor did I ever see A.B. dressed like the man I saw, whether in Miss Gilchrist's house or his own". This, however, is a pure guess. Also, even if it were true, or something like the truth (which is highly doubtful), it is not clear either that Mr. Millar would think it needed to be excised, or that the police would find themselves called upon to discuss possible visits by Lambie to the murderer's house. Inspecting the other asterisks is even more like trying to read in a blackened room than the above. (I would also, as a matter of fact, think it grossly unlikely that Helen Lambie had ever visited A.B.'s house. But perhaps I am being obtuse about the whole episode.)

It was only while rereading the book that I took in the full force of a sentence of Trench's statement which I have already quoted, with regard to Douglas's visit (with Pyper and Dornan) to A.B.'s house on the day after the murder: "I have endeavoured from time to time to elicit what took place in A.B.'s house, but I am without information." The official denial, in 1914, that such a meeting ever took place throws a strange light onto that phrase "from time to time". If the meeting had never happened, one might have anticipated that only one enquiry by Trench would have been needed. As soon as he had been informed that it did not occur, further enquiries would surely not have been possible, or, at least, would not have been warmly received. (We may also note what seems like a discrepancy between Superintendent Ord, on the 24th of April 1914, saying, "I am astonished to hear such a statement made, and I say quite solemnly that it is not true,"—(which is to say, that Trench had returned from Miss Birrell's on the 23rd of December, and had talked of her describing the Lambie outburst about A.B.)—and Miss Birrell herself, saying, one day earlier (23rd April 1914), "have never heard of it being said that I had made such a statement until a few days ago, and it took me completely by surprise." Who, one wonders, had been discussing the case with Miss Birrell "a few days ago"? Under the circumstances, is not Ord's perfectly preserved ignorance a little miracle?

Perhaps the single most interesting point which I took from the book occurred late on, where it gave a long extract from the statement attributed to Helen Lambie which appeared in the Empire News on October the 23rd 1927. (I believe it really is Lambie speaking. If not, it is an utterly brilliant invention) I have already made much of the "scoffing" sentences immediately before it, which runs: "When I told the police the name of the man I thought I recognized they replied "Nonsense! You don't think he could have murdered and robbed your mistress!" They scoffed so much at the notion of this man being etc." Note the "murdered and *robbed*." If the police who interviewed Lambie were convinced they were looking for a man who murdered in the furtherance of attempted robbery, it would make their willingness to laugh off Lambie's identification the more understandable, for it is *a priori* even less credible that a respectable nephew of the deceased should have done this, than that he should have caused her death, most likely by accident, during a heated family argument. Their experience would tell them that this was by no stretch of the imagination a jewel-thief they were dealing with, and (since to them, the one entailed the other) that therefore he could not be the murderer. Having then, miraculously, found the jewel-fancying Slater, whom they knew to be their man, any later suggestion that jewel-theft had nothing whatever to do with it made no retrospective difference to the question of A.B.'s likely guilt or innocence, since by then they *knew* Slater had done it. This seems so plausible

149

an interpretation, that I am a little chagrined not to have thought of it sooner.

About the enquiry itself there is much of interest which I had read and forgotten. For instance, a long letter from David Cook, the lawyer and friend of Trench, to Sir Arthur Conan Doyle, who had already interested himself in the case sufficiently to write a small book, "The Case of Oscar Slater" (published in 1912, as proceedings were being got under way), which graphically shows how different were his expectations of what such an enquiry would involve, from the absurd reality which transpired. (Cook predicted "the Inquiry will be more or less a farce" even before it took place, merely from consideration of its terms. (For instance, no-one was on oath during it.))

Cook still believes, in March 1914, that Miss Birrell will testify to the truth of the statement made to Trench, about what Lambie said to her about A.B. ("Miss Birrell is prepared to swear that Nellie Lambie called at her house at 7:15 P.M. on the night of the murder, entered the house, declared that her mistress had been murdered and that she saw the murderer—naming him. The information was given to the police by Miss Birrell on the night of the murder." This is presumably prior to the astonishing moment (according to her later statement) when she heard all this for the first time.) He makes plain his view of the morality of the upper echelons of the Glasgow police force: "The police were in possession of the facts, and purposely concealed the information from the defense and from the court", and states, "Of course I have complete copies of all the police papers. I am not an optimistic person, but I fail to see how the police can justify their position."

This whole question of the police papers is rather fascinating. From early 1912 Trench had begun to take official files home from police headquarters to study them. (For those who wish to know: it was in April 1912 that the Titanic sank.) Or, rather more than that. According to Cook, "The copies were made by Trench from the originals and I warned him to take numbers of the various Books with the page in each case. He followed my advice." His opinion of the Glasgow police further leads him to surmise, "It is probable that the original documents will be destroyed, although I believe that a little calm reflection will prevent the police acting so foolishly. At the inquiry we can call for the various books describing them by number, page and date. Trench will swear to them."

In fact, there seems to have been no question of calling for documents in open court, and no detailed scrutiny of police records. At the Enquiry, several documents alluded to by Trench were solemnly stated never to have existed. One might assume from this, if one wished, that they had been permanently mislaid, but in fact this would hardly even be necessary, for Mr. Millar seemed willing to accept the truth of this without demur. Look, for instance, at this passage from Ord's testimony: "If Detective Lieutenant Trench states that he supplied to me a statement to him by Miss Birrell on 23rd December 1908, then it should be on the file. I cannot trace such a statement and the numbers on the file are consecutive. With regard to the Copying Books that were used at the time of the murder, the Copying Book in use at the time was near an end and I started a new book in order to keep the statements in the Gilchrist murder together, although finishing off the old book with other cases. When it was necessary to get the papers together for extradition some of the officers' statements were recopied."

As far as I understand this, which I admit is not far, none of these books were ever produced, or even asked to be produced. In short, we have only Superintendent Ord's word for it. My own instinct is to suspect that precautions were taken lest books should be required to be produced, and that all this talk about "starting a new book" and statements being "recopied" is to the highest degree suspicious. Whatever happened, Trench and Cook were not able to call for the various books "describing them by page, number and date". Had they been able to, it would have been fascinating to see what they would have been presented with. I note Cook's remarks in the letter, "I know the Glasgow police better than most people. They know me. I desired them to understand that I was in possession of real information." It is doubtful if this frankness can have done him any good. It largely served to tip his hand to his adversaries. And truly, knowing these men for what they were, did he really suppose, presuming his standpoint to be the true one, that they would docilely turn up at an independent Enquiry, carrying documents that would damn them? A certain amount of judicious "recopying" and "starting a new book" was clearly in order.)

Before leaving Cook's letter, we may glance at its final paragraph. "It occurs to me that it may be necessary later on to approach you on behalf of Trench who may be victimized. I lean to the view that nothing of the kind will happen. If victimization does occur, an outcry will be necessary to prevent injustice to an honest loyal "traitor"." This suggests to me that even Cook, however much of a realist he thought himself to be, did not fully appreciate just the sort of people he was dealing with. (Trench was in fact dismissed without a pension, and subsequently arraigned on a trumped-up charge of reset (along with the unsuspecting Cook), for good measure. Whenever I think I am being too harsh on people like Ord, I remember this charge of reset.)

151

(By the way, we may also remember that several depositions of witnesses, advantageous to Slater, also went missing, before the trial, en route from the police to the law agents. Truly, the Glasgow police at that time seemed to have a lot of trouble with their documents. (A propos nothing, I will add here a sentence which Hunt writes about William Park, author of "The Truth About Oscar Slater": "He had got it into his head (and it must be admitted that events seemed to justify him) that the police were wrong from start to finish, corrupt through and through, perjured, vindictive, irresponsible, callous." This is remarkable not so much for what it says about Park, which is only what everybody else says, but for the bit in parenthesis, which, at a stroke, undercuts much of the careful, there-are-two-sides-to-this approach of the rest of this [Hunt's] book.))

One might think it a further oddity of an enquiry into the truth of a certain state of affairs, if two witnesses give contradictory evidence, yet no attempt is made to determine which, if either, is correct. This is what happens here, with respect to Mary Barrowman and Agnes Brown. One (Mary Barrowman) sees one man run down West Princes Street, and turn left up West Cumberland Street, at the same moment as the other (Agnes Brown), who is actually precisely where, by the other's account, this man should be, (she is walking down West Cumberland Street) sees two men run directly along West Princes Street until they reach Rupert Street, which is two blocks away on the right. Not only is neither witness taken to task, and no awkward questions are asked, but, in his introduction to the report, Mr Millar, heaping praise on almost everybody but Trench, describes Agnes Brown as "very intelligent", and Barrowman "seemed to be honest and anxious to tell the truth" (I recall that Park rips into that last remark.) I sometimes wonder if Mr. Millar ever even realised that there was a discrepancy involved here.

(An intriguing footnote in Hunt's book tells us that "In private, Agnes Brown once confided to a solicitor that attempts had been made in 1909 to get her to see her evidence in a new light so as to suit Barrowman's story". "To see her evidence in a new light". What a beautiful phrase. So much more elegant than "perjury". At this moment I am unaccountably reminded of the anonymous police source quoted by the Weekly Mail as he reacted in astonishment to the news of Slater's reprieve. After much teeth-gnashing, he continues, "the Procurator-Fiscal, Mr. Hart, gave his entire time to the case. Any link in the chain that could in any way be considered weak was removed, and another and stronger one with much care substituted. There was no lack of witnesses, but only those whose testimony could stand the stiffest cross-examination were chosen." (A chain with a weak link in it is, proverbially, a weak chain. To sub-

152

stitute links one must of course first break the chain. I believe this process requires a certain amount of forging to complete it. (Note also that Slater, in custody in January, was not put on trial until the end of May.))

Thus Mr. Hart, forger of links and Procurator-Fiscal for Lanarkshire, plays an interesting part in the narrative. At that time the Procurator-Fiscal worked with the police, rather than acting as an independent arbiter of who should be prosecuted and who not, on evidence forwarded to his office by the police forces. (I believe the Slater case played an important part in effecting this change of emphasis.) There is much evidence that, in this case, Mr. Hart threw himself into his task with an indiscreet amount of enthusiasm. We recall Lambie, at New York, (where, by the way (Q: "Is that man in this room?"—Lambie: "I wouldn't like to say") she showed considerable reluctance to identify Slater) testifying to having sworn to and signed written depositions of testimony in Mr. Hart's office "more times than I could tell you". We recall Mary Barrowman's signed statement (Daily News, Nov. the 5th 1927), given during the final assault after publication of Park's book, to the effect that she was called to Hart's office day after day, to listen to long, pressurizing speeches. ("I want to state most definitely that I thought Mr. Hart's demeanour was not what it should be. He was the party who was laying down what was to be said.") Whatever we may think of the value of Barrowman's original testimony, it can hardly be doubted that if, as she claimed, it was a question of a Procurator-Fiscal, surrounded by the alienating majesty of his office, trying to persuade a 15 year-old message-girl to alter "That man there is very like him" (New York), to "Q: Look at the prisoner; is that the man?" "Yes, that is the man who knocked against me that night" (Trial), she could hardly be expected, in the end, to refuse.

And we also remember Mrs. Liddell (Adams' sister) at the trial, talking about the Watcher's coat. Not merely the "I have stuck to that all along, and I will stick to it still," about its not being a waterproof; but also, as to the colour: "Well, first of all I said browny-fawn, but Mr. Hart seemed to have a good deal of difficulty about browny-fawn [what on earth has Mr. Hart to do with deciding the colour of the coat?], and so I was agreeable that it should pass as a coat the predominant colour of which was brown." Here we have a valuable glimpse of the man at work, fearlessly forging new links in the damning chain. Or, to use a less elegant phrase: doctoring the evidence.

We cannot really leave this disquisition on the Secret Enquiry without quoting Cook's letter (found only in Hunt's book) again to Sir Arthur Conan Doyle, written on the 24th of April, the day after

153

the opening: ". . . Trench was the last witness to be examined for the day. I saw him later on. He is a very shrewd man and absolutely upright. He told me that in his view the inquiry was as big a farce as has been perpetrated for some considerable time in legal circles."

He goes on: "In the first place the Sheriff went for him like a pickpocket: told him that Miss Birrell and Lambie had denied the A.B. matter and would he dare to insist." (Notice that Trench's statement precedes in the report these statements whose substance he insisted on controverting. It seems to me this rather blunts its effect. Trench looks to be denying verbal reports rather than signed, sworn statements. (Well, actually, they are not sworn, but this is easy to forget, and the report does not exactly thrust this into one's field of vision.))

"He replied that he insisted, and produced his Diary which has been kept in first-class order showing that he made the visits." Nothing was said of this production in the report.

"Latterly, Trench had to turn upon the Sheriff and object to being catechized on the question of why he passed over his superiors and consulted me." Nor of this. (One almost wonders why Mr. Millar felt himself obliged to insert asterisks where he did. A certain amount seems to have evaporated anyway, unasterisked.)

Cook predicts the outcome of the Enquiry with accuracy, proposes in that eventuality to publish copies of the relevant documents (presumably those given, only to be dismissed, in the subsequent White Paper based on the Enquiry), and concludes (in Hunt's excerpt) tellingly, and, it seems to me, with complete justification: "To release Slater as a result of the present agitation practically means a censure on the police, on the Fiscal, on the Lord Advocate and on the judge. Rather than have the matter come to the light of day, every effort has been and will be made to burke honest investigation."

Forty-Seven

Truly, it was more than somewhat forward of me to embark on a work about Oscar Slater, knowing so little about him as I did. I think I have already mentioned, long ago, the almost casual origin of this work. Two or three months ago, all I knew about the case had been gleaned from the only two items of literature about the case which I possessed—the Penguin paperback "Famous Trials No. 1" (bought secondhand for 45 pence), which contained the introductions to four of Hodge's series of "Notable British Trials", including the long introduction by William Roughead to the final version of "Oscar Slater". There was also a paperback entitled, "Classic Crimes", also by William Roughead, which I had also bought secondhand (85 pence—curiously, it too was an American edition of the book), and which contained no less than twelve items, including a different look at Slater, evidently written some time after the first.

At some point in the recent past, when already embarked on this, I bought a secondhand copy of the second edition (paperback) of the locally very famous book by Jack House—"Square Mile of Murder"—which had been made into a TV series some time ago. I had already read the relevant parts of this in both editions, but it was worth buying if only for the photographs. (The second edition of this book is remarkable in that it sudenly revealed, like a rabbit pulled out of the hat, a young male called Birrell (presumably also a nephew, like A.B.) who was apparently battering the old lady in while A.B. was rummaging through her private correspondence. This is sensational stuff, but it would be reassuring to know a bit more about him, beyond that, apparently, a relative of his once told Jack House in a pub that all the family knew he had done it. (Particularly since, according to the first edition, exactly the same thing had occurred to him with regard to A.B., even though he did not believe that. (The other man in the pub seems to be the sole reason he gives for believing his later story. But people lie; people play practical jokes; people get drunk. One cannot help feeling that, if the author were to disappear into a pub with a relative of George Bernard Shaw, a third edition of his book would contain a sensational update.)))

(It is this book which baldly states that Maggie Ferguson, the ex-servant, as a contemporary rumour (attested to at the trial by another of Miss Gilchrist's ex-servants) ran, was Miss Gilchrist's illegitimate daughter. This seems to me to be no more plausible than suggesting that Marion Gilchrist and Maggie Ferguson were passionate lovers. (Her husband obviously insisted that they go to live in Kilmarnock, to separate them, and remove her out of temptation's way.)

The fourth and last item of my vast Slater collection is the Hunt book, so recently acquired (paperback—75 pence). My entire library thus consists of four secondhand paperbacks bought for just under £3 in all. Only one of them is entirely about Slater. More curiously, two of them are American. I bought both of these in a shop in Bank Street. This is 10-15 minutes away from the scene of the crime. (And about the same distance from where I live. It is a brief way beyond the Kelvinbridge Underground Station).

The fact that this book has, in a sense, crossed the Atlantic twice, to arrive back almost in the same spot that it started out from, greatly appeals to me. It also makes it clear that I was born in an extremely famous street. How many people are born in streets where events have taken place, discussions of which have been published in popular paperback in the USA? We belong to a select band indeed. Fortune has marked us for her own.

I must also admit that, when I perused the list of the other titles in the series of which "The Great Suspect" formed one, and saw that all bar one of the others were fiction—and that the other exception was entitled "The Madeleine Smith Affair" (also by Peter Hunt)—I felt myself being infused by a sort of insane patriotic pride that the not entirely unGod-forsaken city of Glasgow had produced both of the only two factual accounts thought worthy of inclusion in the series. And that is not even including the M'Lachlan Affair. Truly, no other country has miscarriages of justice that remotely approach our own in quality. Any lesser nation would long ago have been ruined by self-conceit. Why, you can say what you like about Glasgow, but nonetheless the fact remains that etc. etc.

Forty-Eight

It seems to me that I might as well get back to doing what I thought I was doing a while back, and start picking off my notes one by one. However, there are one or two things I should mention first.

I made a polite enquiry to M.L. about the double denial of Lambie's ever having been to Slater's house. Far from it penetrating the central core of his view of the case, he had obviously never before noticed it, and he was content to dismiss it as, in some sense, merely an offshoot of police routine. This is quite probably indeed all there is to it, but it still worries me that I might be missing something of great importance here.

The same evening, I discussed the same point with a couple of friends who know nothing about the case except for a garbled retelling from me. One of them, basing his view on my misinformation, very quickly emerged with the notion that this denial could be a pre-emptive strike by the police against a possible revelation, later in the enquiry from (as far as I understood it) Slater himself, that Lambie had been in his house, which had hitherto for some reason been suppressed. In the real world, this is, I hope, a quite obvious non-starter, but in an information desert it is all too plausible, and it was defended with such tenacity that I was glad when the subject changed before my temper had done more than begin to fray slightly.

At some point between these meetings, I met in the street a young woman whom I know slightly, accompanied only by her child, her husband (whom I also know slightly) being elsewhere. The name of Slater having cropped up in the course of our previous conversation (a few hours earlier—I met her as I was going into, and again after I had come out of, the Mitchell Library), she was now able to tell me why it had sounded vaguely familiar to her. This was because the publishing firm that had put out the second edition of the Jack House book referred to above, had at that time been run by her husband! I have arranged to meet him. I suppose I should have done this before starting to write anything, but that is not how we professionals work.

But to our task. I find among my notes this excerpt: "Dr. Perry, her medical man for several years, had warned her, indeed, not to do so when she was alone in the house." Judging by its position, this is from a newspaper report of the day after the murder, and refers, as far as I recall, to a warning not to answer the door under

157

the above-mentioned circumstances. This throws a new light on the "Detectives Pyper and M'Vicar and Dr. Pirie were in the house when I arrived" of Douglas's statement to the 1914 enquiry. Presumably, a newspaperman talked to Dr. Pirie at the locus, perhaps as he was leaving, induced this recollection of his, and took the name down wrongly. (It is a very easy mishearing.)

Pirie, of course, was not used at the trial. (Neither was Dr. Adams, the first medical man on the scene. I think I have mentioned this before, and how unprecedented it is for the earliest medical witness not to be called at the subsequent trial (his views were most inconvenient for the Prosecution—particularly its absurd hammer theory), but it occurs to me that Douglas does not mention Adams, who presumably had already left by then. (I must check what is said of Adams at the actual trial.)) Apart from anything else, this remark, if repeated, would highlight the improbability of an unknown assailant gaining entrance to the house. Indeed, it argues against anyone who was not already expected gaining entrance, if he arrived after Lambie had left.

(One recalls Edgar Wallace's remark, in the famous review of William Park's book: "As obvious, to my mind, the murderer was in the house when she left." I disagree with this, although I don't dismiss it out of hand. One may note with some suspicion if one wants to Lambie's observing two wet footprints, or her insistence that she closed the outside door, which was ajar at her return. Perhaps these are slightly doubtful factors, but even I, who perhaps suspect too much and too many, would draw the line some way short of this. What? The murderer quarrels with or attacks Miss Gilchrist as soon as Lambie leaves. And then what? Surely it would then be a question of either Lambie's life or his? (Unless, of course, Miss Gilchrist let him in by herself, and Lambie wasn't sure who it was. On Roughead's summary of Lambie's statement of 23rd October 1927 (discussed earlier as excerpted by Hunt (the Empire News is not available in the reference libraries which I can use)), this did at times happen. "She gives interesting particulars of former visits by other men whom her mistress did not allow her to see, Miss Gilchrist letting them in and out of the house herself; and on one occasion she overheard a quarrel between her mistress and one of the occult visitants." Almost at once, however, he tells us, "She says that her mistress sometimes sent her on unimportant errands when one of these covert callers was expected, and that it was not her regular custom to go out nightly for a newspaper". The latter alternative seems to me, in this instance, to be the far more likely one.)

158

Forty-Nine

I must say the more I learn about the case, the more I think I begin to understand something of Lambie's predicament. She is for me now a far more equivocal character than she was when I embarked on this venture. At that time she seemed hardly to be distinguished from a double-dealing liar. Listen to a little more of the Oct. 27th statement: "... there were many circumstances to make it easier for me to accept the notion that Slater was the man ... everybody seemed to know that the police had arrested, or were about to arrest, a man who was a criminal and was capable of almost any crime. Moreover, we were told that he had been caught trying to escape to America with some of the property of my mistress..." Perhaps there is an element of retrospective self-exculpation here, but to me it sounds more likely to be someone whose conscience still troubles her, saying as much as can honestly be said for herself. I believe that this really is Lambie speaking, and that she is speaking the truth.

(Note, for instance, the "one whose life has been a catalogue of crimes" in the interview given by an unnamed member of the police force after the reprieve had been granted. Add to them various graphic remarks by both the Lord Advocate in his summing-up (e.g. "he may be, and probably is, the worst of men" etc.), and the judge in his address to the jury. (It may be pointed out here that Slater did indeed have a criminal record. Ten years previously, he had been involved in a fight in Edinburgh, during which *his own* nose was broken. (Both men were fined twenty shillings.) He had also been found in a gambling club when police had raided it. Fined five shillings.) (And as to the brooch: since the police were famously shy about telling the truth about it even to their counterparts in New York (there are several press reports contemporary with the extradition procedures which clearly still suppose Slater to be in possession of Miss Gilchrist's stolen brooch), we need not over-exercise our credulity by supposing that they were scrupulously specific about it when talking to Lambie.))

This increase in general confidence generates a corresponding increase in one's belief as to the validity of her identification of A.B. Her reluctance to identify Slater at New York, (even after the whole thing had been so elaborately set up (viewings of photographs beforehand, painstaking chance observation in the corridor)) speaks in her favour. Her belief that Slater was a worthless abandoned criminal to *some* degree mitigates her identification of him as Miss Gilchrist's murderer, the more so in that so many people of forbidding power, who presumably whole-heartedly believe him to be guilty (and they should know, shouldn't they?), are subjecting her to pressure to identify him positively.

But, of course, all this only takes us so far and no further. Did she, at any point (as Pyper stated at the Enquiry), claim that she did not think she would be able to identify the man again? If so, when? ("They put into the witness-box to swear against Slater a witness who had already confessed to them that she could not identify the murderer at all." (Park) It takes the breath away. (Particularly if we consider that of the other two star witnesses, one was chronically short-sighted, and the other was probably somewhere else at the time.) We also note, from the same book, "We rather suspect that at this stage Lambie was disinclined to go further and was virtually telling the authorities not to send her." (To New York, that is.) As far as I recall, Park supposes the denial to have been real, but tactical, and certainly not made on the night of the murder. (Perhaps it came as much from exhaustion as anything else. Besides which, one could hardly expect her to switch from identifying A.B. to identifying someone else. She could reasonably have thought that this statement of retraction would be enough to get her out of this nightmare.))

It is normal to attribute Lambie's most characteristic remarks in evidence in New York and Glasgow either to impudence or to downright stupidity. Without wishing to deny her the possible possession of either of these attributes, I think allowance should also be made for the next to impossible position she was in, presumably through none of her own volition. To say that the authorities had manhandled her into the witness-box to lie in their favour is doubtless an exaggeration, but not a great one. She was time and again having to say things that went against her better judgement. I suspect sheer desperation had a lot to do with it.

We may, I think, reasonably suppose that Lambie viewed the prospect of the impending 1914 Enquiry with something less than hysterical enthusiasm. We may also note that, if Lambie and Miss Birrell were to corroborate Trench's claims, then things would get uncomfortably hot for the leading lights of the Glasgow police.

Does it, I wonder, make sense for us to embark on a slight detour here, and ask what the likelihood ever was that Lambie and Miss Birrell would choose to back Trench up? Cook's letter seems to suggest that Miss Birrell had recently expressed a willingness to do so. But, reflect for a moment. For Lambie to agree to Trench's deposition would require that she admit that she incriminate many of the major figures in the Glasgow police. For Miss Birrell to agree would at least require her to tend to displace the guilt from the back of a shady, unknown foreigner, onto one of her young male relatives. It seems to me that this presents distinctly fertile ground for anyone wishing to cultivate a little judicious and judicial forgetfulness.

Nonetheless, it may be that Lambie, conscious by now that she was not utterly without power, extracted some sort of quid pro quo for her collaboration. Thus we have the repeated testimony as to her good character. It may also be (a sheer guess) that one of the many rumours circulating in the wake of the case that particularly distressed Lambie was one to the effect that she had known and visited Slater prior to the murder, and that her nervousness was somewhat soothed by the reassurance that this would be denied at the highest level. (Perhaps it was something which the police had at one time suggested to her was the case, and she was merely making sure, to safeguard herself entirely from any possible repetition of this, that they put their rejection of this theory definitively on the record. (Of course, all this only stresses how important it was for a rigorous, judicial enquiry to have been constituted instead of the charade that took place.))

As it was, shortly after the enquiry (in 1916, I think) Lambie and her husband went to the USA (Madeleine Smith definitely emigrated to the USA in 1916, at the age of 80. Jessie M'Lachlan had already died in that country, long before, in 1899. The journey of the interesting female to the USA seems to be a cliche of the genre.) This may have been prompted by the desire to be closer to Charlie Chaplin, but other, more plausible motives spring to mind. That she refused to return for the Slater Appeal in 1928 will, I trust, surprise no-one. The chief reason for her very being in America was presumably to get away from such things and start afresh. (It seems she actually went into hiding at this time. (Why do I find myself wondering where she got the fare for the journey?)) Her much-quoted remark on hearing of the quashing of the conviction—"Thank God it is all over"—is perhaps as much a reference to what she herself had been going through for the last twenty years, as to what Slater had been going through. (She was still only slightly over 40.) It must often have occurred to her how different it would all have been if she had only not applied for that job, but for the one above it or the one below it instead. Or if some other, luckier female had pipped her to it. After all, why should the various secret problems of the Gilchrists ever have concerned her in the first place?

Fifty

I have just been making discreet enquiries into the biography and character of the leading suspect in the case—which is to say, the man traditionally referred to as A.B. Looking up the name in the Post Office Glasgow Directory of 1909 the occupant of the address which my journalist gave me, I discover not merely the anticipated Dr. Charteris, again strangely precise among all the unknown names, now I find out his first name: to wit, Frank. *(I guiltily recall slipping it into this work earlier, unannounced, for dramatic effect, but this must be where I discovered it for the first time.)*

This sent me scurrying down to the relevant "Who Was Whom"— an invalauable work of reference which somehow I have never used in my entire life. It tells me, and anyone else who cares to peruse it, of a Francis James Charteris (F.J., it strikes me, also are my initials), M.D., LL.D., Emeritus Professor of Materia Medica at St. Andrew's University. Every word of this seems to proclaim "He could not possibly have done it" loud and clear. He was the second son of another M.D., Mathew Charteris, the Professor of Materia Medica and Therapeutics at Glasgow University from 1880-97. (It seems to me that, if all this is to fit together, his mother must be a sister of Miss Gilchrist's. (Presumably a copy of his birth certificate—5th Dec. 1875—would clinch this. A more committed researcher than I would at once drop everything else until he had found this out.))

He was, we note, a second son. This elder brother is, as far as I know, unknown to history. The man himself was educated at Glagow and Leipzig Universities. (Leipzig, of course, is impressively near to Slater's birthplace, but countless medical students must have gone there in that era.) He married, in 1907, the year before the murder, Annie Fraser, M.A., the eldest daughter of a Justice of the Peace (apparently one Robert Kedie, J.P., D.L.—I don't quite understand this. Is the daughter's surname Fraser and the father's Kedie?)

I must say, shame-facedly, that it never occurred to me before that A.B. was married. Neither had I thought him quite so respectable. Where, one asks, was his wife on the night of Dec. 21st 1908? (Strange indeed that, 77 years later, we should find ourselves asking such a question.) One presumes she was at home. This puts him instantly within the reach of alibi, even if it is actually no better than Slater's was. He made, we learn, "numerous contributions to medical journals". He died on the 4th of July 1964, that day of many distant

162

fireworks.

This, then, is the man whom Lambie named, or so the story runs. It makes the obsessiveness of the protection surrounding him the more understandable, in that such an accusation could shatter a distinguished career. (Of course, if he had actually done it, it might be thought his career should suffer just a little.) Lo and behold, he turns out to be a real doctor.

But what of Lambie's part in all this? Did she simply mistake him for someone else? (Of course, I mean the reverse.) Yet, he had visited more than once. He seems already to have been a known figure in that locality. And why was he visiting? Familial concern? He was, after all, not her doctor. I have nowhere seen the suggestion made that he was treating her for any ailment. If an intelligent man, used to dealing with death, did indeed walk out past Adams at the door, then suspicion cannot but remain strong. Much turns on Lambie's identification. As things stand, I can do nothing more here, except perhaps mention that the Watcher seemed to put in his first appearance very close to this man's 33rd birthday, which, of course, suggests very little and proves even less.

(I found, by the way, as I casually scanned the Post Office Glasgow Directory, that in 1908-1910 there lived at 69 West Princes Street, perhaps five doors away from Miss Gilchrist, one Robert Perry, M.D. This is obviously Miss Gilchrist's own doctor (it was a popular residential district for doctors), and it is Douglas's statement, talking of a Dr. Pirie, which is presumably the inaccurate one, and not the newspaper report's. Inevitably, I find myself wondering what age Dr. Perry was, and whether perhaps Lambie merely mistook one doctor for another, but this is what prolonged exposure to the Slater case does to you. I think it would be better for everyone if I stopped soon.)

Fifty-One

To return for a moment to the absolutely endless Helen Lambie affair: it disconcerts me to have to admit it (this is one of the consequences of not having the relevant books to hand) but in fact Lambie herself was seemingly questioned at length about a possible connection with Slater, during her appearance before the 1914 Enquiry. After denying that her discussion with Trench, just after the New Year (what a New Year celebration that must have been!) had anything to do with A.B., her signed statement continues as follows: "I did not know Oscar Slater before the night of the murder. I never saw him before that. I never saw him in company with a man named Nugent. I was not in Oscar Slater's house; I didn't even know where he lived. I had nothing whatever to do with Slater previous to the murder and knew nothing about him." She then, after four or five unequivocally true consecutive sentences (a rarity at the Enquiry, it sometimes seems) gets back onto the old track by denying that she ever at any point mentioned A.B. to anyone.

This strongly suggests that the harping on A.B. came courtesy of Mr. Millar himself. (Almost certainly the suggestion that it somehow originated from Lambie can be quietly put to sleep here. *(Actually, I would like to wake it up again. Surely it would be only to be expected that Lambie herself would welcome the opportunity to clear her name in explicit terms? But perhaps I am missing something too obvious to my earlier self—who was so much better-informed than I—to need mentioning then.)* Nugent, once a very obvious suspect, is a former flame of Lambie's. Indeed, it seems he was once even so favoured as to be allowed to have tea with Lambie and Miss Gilchrist when they were on holiday at the coast. He often visited the house.

His name came up at the trial, where he received publicly a clean bill of health from all and sundry. It is interesting to see him reappear here, nonetheless, in company with Slater. And again the suggestion that she might have been in Slater's house. How is this suggestion part of the case? (By the way, Slater, when in prison, knowing of course only what he had heard at the trial, and desperately trying to make sense of what was a complete mystery to him, wrote a letter to his law agents suggesting they investigate Nugent as a likely culprit. (Or, perhaps, the only other possible named culprit. (He seems, after the trial, to disappear from Lambie's life at a run. I suspect

Miss Birrell's reference at the 1914 Enquiry to Lambie's sweetheart as being "a collier" (presumably Gillon, her eventual husband) is slightly anticipatory, but this is a mere hunch.)) One gets a glimpse of Slater, utterly baffled, in prison for a crime which he knew nothing about, except for those details which he had learned during a trial at which, mystifyingly, he was the accused.)

Quite possibly I am making a mountain out of a molehill here, but these Lambie/Slater suggestions do not, I think, occur in Trench's submission, and, if not, what is Mr. Millar doing devoting so much time to them? I don't know. Is he following up a pet theory of his own? Surely not. (He does not strike me as even being *capable* of forming a theory of his own. (And, while on the subject of Lambie, I may as well clear up here a newspaper snippet I took down: "Lambie admitted that her nerves thereafter completely broke down." This is her talking to a reporter on the actual night of the murder. Her nerves have apparently by now recovered. It seems to me possible that this shows her already forced into a position of having to steer a treacherous course between what she actually thought she saw, and what, for one reason or another, she was constrained to claim she saw. (It is possible that we have her here laying the ground for retracting a claim about A.B., or for explaining how she could possibly ever have said such a thing. (How was she to know the police would be such a big help?) Or it may simply be a more general escape route being laid. Or, of course, it may simply have been the truth. Possibly, normal human nerves are *meant* to break down under such circumstances as these.) I suppose that from that moment when she climbed up the narrow short stairways for the unconsidered X-hundred-and-Yth time, and was astonished to see Adams there, who, in her experience, never visited Miss Gilchrist (and certainly would never again have the opportunity (her surprise, by the way, implies that she had not seen him enter the doorway of No. 49, although she must have been fairly near, and was approaching all the time along the pavement with a habitual newspaper)) her life was horribly changed into someone else's. (Thinking back to the numerous contemporary reports which had Adams climbing up to Miss Gilchrist's to placate the old lady's fears. It is possible there is good deal of journalistic embroidery here. But it is also possible that Adams would be most needed when Miss Gilchrist was quite without company, and therefore particularly susceptible to frights. Alas, I have no idea how often, if ever, Lambie slept out of the house, leaving the old lady alone and afraid. There would really be no reason, would there, for anyone to tell her that Adams had had to come upstairs to placate the old lady's fears on such and such a night.)))

Fifty-Two

I might as well mention here that, a week or two ago, I bought a copy of the volume in the "Notable British Trials" series, devoted to that of Mary Queen of Scots. It had a piece missing from the top of the spine, and was thus offered for sale ridiculously cheap. The book itself is somewhat forbidding to read, being chiefly in Latin and late medieval English, but it did enough to merit the expenditure merely by providing, as an insert at the end of the volume, an advertising supplement from the publishers, wherein the other works in this inestimable, if somewhat diabolic, series, are described in brief paragraphs of great interest. The series of course includes "The Trial of Oscar Slater" (1909).

Now, the Mary Queen of Scots book was published in 1923. Slater has been in prison for 14 years. (Curiously enough, Mary Queen of Scots herself was in effect in prison for the last 18 years of her life, which was the same length of time, to within a few months, as that which Slater spent incarcerated. The sheer duration of Slater's spell is slightly disguised by the fact that he lived for another 20 years after his release. (As to where we would all be if Slater had quietly and obediently died in prison in, say, 1923, well, God only knows; but it seems clear that, until very late on, it was the official intention to leave him there for ever. (He was, from the offical point of view, a bad prisoner. Not only did he keep on protesting his innocence, but he also saw fit to report the wardens if their maltreatment of other prisoners came to his attention. Truly, a born troublemaker. (It was fairly normal for a "lifer" to have his position reviewed after a set period, when he could, subject to official approval, be released on license. Needless to say, no such thing ever happened to Slater, but it is conceivable that the merely possibility of this happening went some way to sustaining him through the long personal silence that succeeded the Enquiry. (The usual period was fourteen years. Which is to say, in Slater's case, 1923—when the Mary Queen of Scots book was published.)))))

"The case of Oscar Slater, who was tried in May 1909, for the murder of Miss Marion Gilchrist, excited widespread interest at the time, and, by reason of the sensational rumours of which it was the occasion, exercised the popular imagination for many months," the blurb begins. It continues: "But apart from these, the case itself contains elements sufficiently strange and suggestive to supply, in